SELF-MANAGEMENT
&
GOAL SETTING

Douglas Gordon

Career Solutions Training Group
Paoli, PA

VISIT US ON THE INTERNET
www.swep.com
www.thomson.com

South-Western
Thomson Learning™

Cincinnati • Albany, NY • Belmont, CA • Bonn • Boston • Detroit • Johannesburg • London • Madrid
Melbourne • Mexico City • New York • Paris • Singapore • Tokyo • Toronto • Washington

Peter McBride: Vice President/Director of Publishing
Eve Lewis: Team Leader
Laurie Wendell: Project Manager
Alan Biondi: Editor
Patricia Matthews Boies: Production Coordinator
Kathy Hampton: Manufacturing Coordinator
Mark Linton: Marketing Manager
Tricia Allen: Marketing Coordinator
Dr. Carolyn Love: National Career Development/Communication Consultant

Thanks to the following educators and trainers
who provided valuable assistance during the development of the QUICK SKILLS materials:

Robert W. Moses
Vice President for Planning and Program Development
Indian River Community College
Fort Pierce, Florida

Richard Winn
Director, Educational Projects
Heald Colleges
San Francisco, California

Debra Mills
Education-to-Careers/Tech Prep Director
Danville Area Community College
Danville, Illinois

Patrick Highland
Director of Vocational Education
Iowa City Community School District
Iowa City, Iowa

Julie Kibler
Business Teacher and Business Department Chairperson
Castle High School
Newburgh, Indiana

Dave Hyslop
External Liaison
Bowling Green State University
Bowling Green, Ohio

Dr. Doris Humphrey: Project Manager
Deborah Stuart: Production Editor
Pam Dooley: Typography

13 East Central Avenue, Paoli, PA 19301
Telephone: 1-888-299-2764 • FAX: (610) 993-8249
E-mail: cstg@bellatlantic.net • Website: www.careersolutionsgroup.com

CONTENTS

This book is about the art of managing yourself. You may wonder what that means and what relevance it has to you.

Think of it this way: Some elements in your life are pretty much beyond your control. Your job may require you to work certain hours. If you're taking classes, you probably don't control when the class meets and what assignments you have to complete. When you earn money, the government requires you to pay taxes. It's hard to change matters like that.

But there are plenty of elements in your life that you can control, and self-management means taking charge of those elements. Too often, in this hectic world, it seems like everyday events are controlling us. The workshops in this book will help *you* get in control.

A major part of self-management is goal setting—that is, figuring out what you really want to do in your life. Once you become clear about your goals, you can take effective action to realize them. Self-management also involves setting priorities for yourself, getting organized, and managing your time.

Do the following self-assessment to see where you stand on some of the issues in self-management. For each statement, mark the response that best applies to you.

	Often	Sometimes	Never
1. I'm not really clear about my main goals in life.	❏	❏	❏
2. In terms of making big improvements in my life, I feel like I'm getting nowhere.	❏	❏	❏
3. Important things in my life have to be postponed because there's so much that's absolutely urgent.	❏	❏	❏
4. Thinking about the work I have to do makes me feel snowed under.	❏	❏	❏
5. People pile an unfair amount of work on me.	❏	❏	❏
6. It's hard to concentrate because I get interrupted so many times.	❏	❏	❏
7. I feel frustrated because there isn't enough time for the things I most want to do.	❏	❏	❏
8. With tasks I don't like, I put them off till the last minute.	❏	❏	❏
9. Big projects can overwhelm me.	❏	❏	❏
10. I tend to run late.	❏	❏	❏

How many times did you mark "Sometimes" or "Often"? If you gave these responses even once, you'll likely benefit from studying self-management techniques.

As you begin the workshops in this book, there's one encouraging principle to keep in mind. It's often called the *law of the slight edge*. The difference between success and failure, the law says, is usually just a matter of a slight edge. Think about the 100-meter dash in the Olympics. What's the time difference between the gold medal winner and the fourth-place finisher?

Usually just a few tenths of a second. The winner had a slight edge in training or skill that produced a huge difference in results.

What you read in this book will probably not bring you an Olympic gold medal. But in your daily pursuits self-management can give you the slight edge that makes all the difference between failure and success. With the right self-management techniques, instead of feeling like events are controlling you, you can take charge and begin to feel good about your accomplishments.

The phone on Maria's desk is ringing as she rushes back from the photocopier. She grabs the receiver with her left hand while balancing sixteen copies of a report with her right. "Good morning," she says, "CompSupply Computer Products."

The caller asks for Judy Morgan. As Maria sets the copies on the edge of her desk, she punches the hold button and dials Judy's extension. Meanwhile, on her computer screen she sees the itinerary she has been trying to work out for Andy Stepanich's big sales trip. Andy has told her he needs all the information by 11:30. It is now 11:05, and she is still waiting for a travel agent to call her back about some crucial details.

Before Judy Morgan can answer, another phone line begins to flash. "Could that be the travel agent?" Maria wonders, but she can't answer the second call while she's ringing Judy. In frustration she raps her knuckles on the desk. Then, to her horror, she sees the stack of photocopies start to slide. In an instant the papers scatter across the floor. "No!" she yells.

Soon Maria has these small crises under control. But as she heads out to pick up lunch, she feels tired and discouraged.

"I took this entry-level job," she thinks, "because they told me it could lead to a sales position. If I work hard and learn about the company's products and customers, they'll promote me. But how can I learn anything new while I'm in a frazzle all day just trying to keep up? I like the company, but at this rate I'll *never* get ahead."

What's Inside

In these pages, you will learn to:

Short-Term Versus Long-Term Goals

Does Maria's predicament sound familiar? What would you do if you were in her shoes? Think especially about what you know of her *goals*—that is, what she hopes to do with her life.

One way of looking at a problem like Maria's is to see it as a conflict between short-term and long-term goals. In the long run, as you saw, Maria wants to be a salesperson. Perhaps, even further in the future, she dreams of being an executive in the company. On the other hand, she has short-term goals like finishing Andy Stepanich's itinerary and getting the report copied and distributed. Her dilemma is that the immediate, short-term goals seem to prevent her from working toward her long-term goals.

It's a common problem. In today's fast-paced world, we all have too much to do and not enough time to do it. For that reason, we often neglect our long-term goals. Of course, this reduces our chances of reaching those important objectives. We also tend to feel frustrated, angry with ourselves, or angry at others who we may think are standing in our way.

Know Thyself

The first step in resolving goal conflicts is to make clear for yourself what your long-term goals really are. That's the focus of this workshop. Then in the next workshop you'll learn how to reconcile the long term with the short term.

Your long-term goals may not be things you think about every day, especially if they are "on the back burner" in your life right now. But it's important to define them for yourself. Activity 1.1 will help you begin.

Common expressions

Think about the number of ways we have of saying that a potentially important project is being ignored:

"It's on the back burner."
"It got buried."
"It's on hold right now."
"It fell through the cracks."
"It got lost in the shuffle."
"We let it slide."

Can you think of any other such expressions that you hear often?

> " If you don't know where you're going, you'll end up someplace else. "
>
> —Yogi Berra

Checking Your Own Back Burner

As a first step in identifying your long-term goals, look at your own back burner—the things you've been meaning to get to, the tasks you want to accomplish but have been putting off.

Some of these matters may be trivial—washing your car, for instance. But others are probably important. List a few of the biggest and most important items on your back burner:

1. _____

2. _____

3. _____

4. _____

5. _____

A Personal Mission Statement

You may have seen mission statements drawn up by businesses and other organizations. They define the group's essential purpose—why it exists and what it hopes to accomplish. Sometimes you'll find mission statements posted on the wall in a store, a social service agency, or a doctor's office.

Many experts in motivation believe it's useful to apply the same idea at a personal level. That is, as a way of defining your most important goals, you can write your own mission statement.

Hal Lancaster, a writer for the *Wall Street Journal*, composed the following mission statement with the aid of his readers:

My mission is to enlighten and entertain people through my writing and to help provide a life for my family that is emotionally and financially secure, loving, learning and fun.

Here's another example, written by a teacher:

I will seek always to be a learner, exploring new interests and expanding my horizons. As a teacher, I will strive to help all my students develop a passion for learning, think creatively and critically, and become active, productive members of our society.

As these examples show, your mission statement doesn't need to be long. In fact, making it short and to the point may help you focus on the issues that matter most to you.

Getting Started on Your Mission Statement

To begin working on a personal mission statement, see if any of the back-burner items you identified in Activity 1.1 are major enough to relate to your life's mission. Also ask yourself questions like these:

What are my most important values and beliefs, the ones that guide nearly everything I do?

_____

What are my greatest talents?

_____

What do I want more than anything else?

_____

At the end of my life, what would I like to be remembered for?

_____

How will I work toward fulfilling my aims in life?

_____

_____

Brainstorming your way to a mission statement

If you have a hard time coming up with ideas for a mission statement, try _brainstorming_.

✓ Take a clean sheet of paper and write at the top a question like "What Do I Want to Accomplish in Life?"

✓ For a set period of time—say, five minutes—jot on the paper any answer that comes into your head. Think about what you like doing, where you'd like to be in five or ten years, what you'd like to have.

✓ Don't judge what you're writing, just keep going. If one idea leads to another, that's fine. If the ideas seem completely random, that's fine, too.

✓ At the end of your set time, take a short rest and clear your mind.

✓ Now sort through the ideas you've written. Circle the ones that seem most important. See how they connect with one another.

✓ With the words and phrases you've circled, you have some key ideas that can help you state your goals clearly.

Writing Your Mission Statement

Drafting

Using your ideas from Activities 1.1 and 1.2, write a draft of your personal mission statement. Don't be worried if the first attempt doesn't sound perfect. Anything you put down is a good start.

_____

_____

_____

_____

_____

_____

Feedback

When you have finished your draft, show it to a friend, co-worker, or classmate. Ask for reactions and constructive criticism. Summarize the main comments you receive:

_____

_____

_____

_____

_____

_____

Revising

Think about the feedback you have received, and then revise your statement.

_____

_____

_____

_____

_____

_____

You can find more examples of personal mission statements on the World Wide Web. Try entering the phrase *personal mission statement* in an on-line search engine and see what you discover.

(Note: When you're searching for an entire phrase, follow the rules of the particular search engine you are using. Generally you need to put the phrase in "double quotation marks." With some search engines, though, you can use the menu to specify a phrase search.)

For further help with your mission statement, you can try the on-line FranklinCovey Mission Statement Builder, which lets you choose key phrases to describe yourself and the things you value. After you make your choices, it automatically constructs a rough draft of a mission statement for you. Look for it at one of the following World Wide Web sites:

http://www.covey.com/customer/missionform.html
http://www.ivillage.com/career/

You may need to supply a name and e-mail address to log on.

Putting Your Goals in Order

After drafting your personal mission statement, you should have some clearer ideas about your goals in life, but that is only the first step. To begin to act on your goals, you need to put them in a definite order. For one thing, you should think about their relative degrees of importance to you. Perhaps you want to get married, have children, and own a motorcycle—but is the motorcycle as important as the children?

You also need to identify the time frame in which you hope to realize each goal. The reason should be obvious:

Things that don't have to be done by a certain time seldom actually get done, do they? They stay on the back burner forever. So, as you do the next activity, be sure to put a date on each of your goals.

?

Did you know

According to a survey by Day-Timers, the goals expressed by U.S. workers include these:

♦ Getting more exercise	78%
♦ Spending more time with family	65%
♦ Eating better	59%

Your Goals: Time and Rank

Use the form below to list several long-term goals. Include personal as well as career objectives. Maybe you have a goal of getting a certain position at work. Perhaps your other goals include buying a house, earning an educational degree, or becoming fluent in a foreign language.

Write down also how long you will need to reach each goal (three years? five years? ten?). Then, after thinking about how important these goals are to you, rank them in relation to one another.

	My Goal	Time Needed to Reach Goal	Rank (1 = Most Important; 5 = Least Important)
a.			
b.			
c.			
d.			
e.			

Criteria for your goals

To state your goals in the most useful way, try to meet the following criteria:

✓ *Realistic.* Your goals should be things you can actually accomplish.

✓ *Challenging.* Your goals should require you to make an effort.

✓ *Compelling.* Your goals should represent what you are most eager to achieve.

✓ *Positive.* Your goals will be most useful if they are expressed in encouraging terms, such as "Get physically fit" rather than "Stop being a couch potato." Being negative won't help you.

Goals in a Career Field

Select a career field, either one in which you are currently working or one that interests you for the future. Are you attracted to retail sales? Nursing? Teaching?

Get together with a classmate or co-worker who is interested in the same field or a similar one. Discuss your goals as they relate to this type of career. Do you find that the two of you have similar goals or different ones? Do the other person's ideas about the field change the way you look at it? Whose goals seem more realistic?

Use the lines below to summarize what you learn.

My Goal	Other Person's Goal	Comments on Similarity or Difference

WORKSHOP WRAP-UP

- Long-term goals are the big things we want to accomplish in our lives.
- We also have short-term goals—more immediate tasks that we want or need to accomplish—and these sometimes conflict with our long-term goals.
- The first step in resolving the conflict is to define our long-term goals clearly.
- Writing a personal mission statement is a good way to express the broad goals that are most important to us.
- Once we have defined our major purposes in life, we can break them down into individual goals and set a time frame for achieving each one.

Jason dashes up Mrs. Alioto's steps and punches the doorbell, shivering in the cold wind. He has left the drugstore's van double-parked because Mr. Braithwaite, his boss, has already called on the cell phone to tell him to hurry back.

Jason jabs the doorbell again and raps on the door. Braithwaite's, a popular family pharmacy, serves a wide area, and some of the older people like to have their prescriptions delivered. Naturally it's Jason, the new part-timer, who has to do the dashing around in all kinds of weather.

Jason bangs on the door again. Some of these old people have trouble hearing. He tries not to be impatient, but if a police officer sees the van double-parked he may get a ticket, plus a long lecture from the boss.

As he huddles on the doorstep, Jason thinks about his dream of getting into real estate like his older cousin Randall. Driving here, he saw Randall's name on three "For Sale"

signs. Randall is making a career for himself while Jason is turning blue on doorsteps for minimum wage.

At last the gray-haired, slow-moving Mrs. Alioto shuffles to the door. But when she takes her package she questions Jason about one bottle of pills. Is it okay to take this new prescription along with her others? Will it upset her stomach?

"How should I know?" Jason wants to yell at her. "I'm just the delivery guy!" Luckily, however, he keeps his temper and advises her to call Mr. Braithwaite. As he runs back to the van he is shaking his head, convinced that this job is getting him nowhere fast.

Taking Advantage of Opportunities

After doing Workshop 1, you understand Jason's basic problem: The job he has now seems irrelevant to his long-term goals. He spends too much of his time doing work he considers trivial and unproductive. But before agreeing with him that delivering prescriptions has nothing to do with real estate, consider these points:

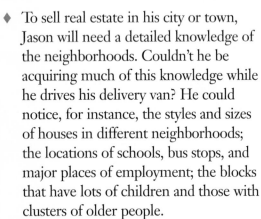

- To sell real estate in his city or town, Jason will need a detailed knowledge of the neighborhoods. Couldn't he be acquiring much of this knowledge while he drives his delivery van? He could notice, for instance, the styles and sizes of houses in different neighborhoods; the locations of schools, bus stops, and major places of employment; the blocks that have lots of children and those with clusters of older people.
- If he goes into real estate, Jason will likely be driving clients around town. He can certainly use his experience in the van to learn the best routes.
- The real estate profession depends heavily on people skills—getting along with clients, listening to their problems, helping them find solutions. Doesn't dealing with Mrs. Alioto give Jason some practice in those skills?

Maybe you can suggest other overlaps between Jason's current job and the profession he hopes to join. Think, too, about ways for him to follow up after working hours. What if, driving around town, he jotted down the addresses of houses for sale, and later that evening he looked up their prices in the newspaper? Wouldn't that build his knowledge of the real estate market?

The point is: We can often take significant strides toward meeting our long-term goals just by making full use of our daily experiences. The following activity will help you apply this idea to your own life.

? Did you know

In a survey conducted by *USA Today*, a third of the respondents admitted that they sometimes took sick days at work when they were not ill but merely "sick of working" or wanted to do something else.

How do you think most of these people see their work in relation to their long-term goals? How much would their behavior change if they found more daily opportunities for making progress toward their goals?

Identifying Your Own Opportunities

Pick two or three of your important long-term goals that you identified in Workshop 1. Think carefully about how your current activities—in work, education, or personal life—relate to each goal. What skills or knowledge are you developing now that you will use later?

Future Goal   **Present Activities That Will Help Me Achieve It**

a. _____   _____

_____

_____

b. _____   _____

_____

_____

c. _____   _____

_____

_____

Keith Ellis's "Magic Lamp" approach

In his book *The Magic Lamp*, Keith Ellis uses the acronym **LAMP** to stand for the following principles in setting and achieving personal goals:

1. **L**ock on: Decide what you want and lock onto it in the same way that a missile locks onto its target.

2. **A**ct: Take appropriate steps to make your desires come true.

3. **M**anage your progress: Keep track of how you're doing and make adjustments in your approach as necessary.

4. **P**ersist: Keep at it! Don't get discouraged.

Turning Long-Term into Short-Term Goals

Activity 2.1 should have helped you find links between your current life and your long-term goals. There's another important lesson in that activity: Progress toward your goals, however lofty they are, can be accomplished in relatively small and simple ways.

The key to acting on your long-term goals is to understand what intermediate steps you need to take to achieve them—the skills or knowledge you need to acquire, the resources you need to find, the help you need from others, and so forth. Then you can break those steps themselves down into smaller, manageable tasks.

For instance, if you're fascinated with Japanese culture and your goal is to find a job with an organization that promotes cultural exchanges between the United States and Japan, an obvious intermediate step is to learn the Japanese language. You can break that down into smaller tasks such as (a) finding out where and when you can take classes in Japanese and (b) finishing up other commitments that would prevent you from taking such a class.

By this process you turn the *future* into *today*. Those big long-range goals that you couldn't deal with become smaller, doable chores, and before you know it, you're making progress!

> " When you divide long-term goals into a series of sub-goals, and then begin achieving the sub-goals, each achievement bolsters your confidence and encourages you to do more. "
>
> —George Sullivan, *Work Smart, Not Hard*

Finding time

All right, you may be grumbling, I can break my long-range goals into smaller tasks, but that still doesn't give me time to work on them. I'm run ragged just keeping up with everyday demands. How can I possibly fit in anything more?

In Workshops 5 and 6 we'll go into the process of time management in more detail. For now, here are a couple of suggestions:

✓ Set aside a specific block of time each day or each week for actions related to your long-term goals. It doesn't need to be a big block of time. Even half an hour or fifteen minutes can help. Just make sure you use the time for that purpose.

✓ Look for small gaps in time in which you could be doing something productive. What do you do when you have half an hour, say, between classes or job assignments? When you expect that you'll sit waiting awhile in a doctor's or dentist's office, do you take along something you need to read?

Step by Step

Let's try breaking long-term goals into short-term steps to see how it works. Choose one of the most important personal goals that you have identified. Write down what you need to do to achieve that goal. Note any obstacles that stand in your path. Then list the practical, doable tasks that you can begin *today*.

Goal _____

What I Need to Achieve It _____

_____

Obstacles to Achieving It _____

_____

Tasks I Can Begin Now:

a. _____

b. _____

c. _____

d. _____

e. _____

GETTING CONNECTED

For more advice on defining your goals in specific, realistic terms, check out the Mind Tools World Wide Web site at the following address:

http://www.mindtools.com/

Under the category "Skills for High Performance Living," the Mind Tools site offers information on goal setting and many of the other topics of this book.

Or try developing your own "goal map" at Goalmap.com:

http://www.goalmap.com/

Staying on Track

The phrase "staying on track" derives originally from railroads, but it has remained in our language through the age of automobiles and airplanes. Could it be that the phrase is still so common because most of us have a tendency to get "sidetracked"?

You've seen how you can work toward your long-term goals by breaking them down into smaller steps that you can take every day and every week. Yet—let's admit it—the process of taking small steps every day is easier to talk about than to accomplish. You can read a complete encyclopedia—and gain a huge amount of knowledge—if you take it just a page a day. Surely that's a manageable daily task. But are you going to do it? Not likely. If you're like most people, you'd probably get sidetracked by day three.

The reason is that reading a whole encyclopedia is probably not crucial to your plans. But your long-term goals are important to you—they're *your* goals, after all—and if you've done a thoughtful job of breaking them into short-term stages, then those smaller steps are important as well.

Keep reminding yourself of your ultimate purpose. You've heard of the famous athletes who practiced eight or ten hours a day when they were young. Obviously they grew tired and discouraged at times, but they kept their goals in mind, and that focus helped them stay on track.

Here are three other strategies for staying on track toward your goals:

Make a timetable. Once you've identified the tasks you can begin today, set up a timetable for getting them done. Don't allow yourself to drift. If the task is to learn Japanese, for instance, you might give yourself a week to find out about the available classes, and then a week to choose one. Write down dates and stick to them.

Do something every day. Don't let a day go by without making some progress, even if the step you take is so tiny that it hardly seems worth taking. The psychological gain can be tremendous.

> **The secret of success is constancy to purpose.**
>
> —Benjamin Disraeli

Be firm with yourself but flexible in your approach. Your timetable won't do much good if you don't stick to it. You need to persevere. But if you find your progress isn't what you expected, you don't have to abandon your plan completely. Rather, think it over, figure out what went wrong, and change your tactics or your timetable accordingly.

Making a Timetable

Select a long-term project from work or home that needs to be done. Set a completion deadline for it if you don't already have one. Now break it down into smaller steps and specific tasks. List them one by one, and set up a timetable for all of them.

Task	Start Date	Finish Date
1. _____	_____	_____
2. _____	_____	_____
3. _____	_____	_____
4. _____	_____	_____
5. _____	_____	_____
6. _____	_____	_____

Now ask yourself: Is this timetable realistic? If not, revise it. When you decide that it is realistic, try it!

WORKSHOP WRAP-UP

- More than we commonly realize, our daily experiences can be valuable in achieving our long-term goals—if we make full use of them.
- The key to making progress toward long-term goals is to break them into shorter, manageable steps that we can take day by day.
- To help yourself stay on track, keep your goals in mind, make a timetable, and do something every day. When problems arise, be firm with yourself, but don't be afraid to modify your approach when necessary.

3 WORKSHOP

Julie turns in bed and shades her eyes from the light streaming through the window. Then something registers in her mind: Why is it so bright? Did I oversleep again?

From her clock she discovers that it's 8:10. She has a chemistry class at 8:30! She pulls on some clothes and rushes to the kitchen.

"Did you sleep through your alarm?" her roommate asks. "I thought I heard it go off an hour ago. You got in pretty late last night, huh?"

Julie snatches a muffin from the counter and calls, "See you later."

Driving to her chemistry class, Julie smiles to herself. Of course she was out late—her good friend Vanessa was in town for the first time in three months. Although it meant giving up sleep and postponing some work, she needed to get together with Vanessa.

Julie is taking chemistry so that she can apply to veterinary school. She has always liked animals, and she dreams of a career as an animal doctor. Today, luckily, she arrives only five minutes late for class, though when Mr. Davis calls on her she isn't prepared because she didn't have time to finish the assignment. "Look," he says sternly, "I expect all of you to prepare for this class. It should be a high priority."

That afternoon, Julie goes to her job as an assistant at the local veterinary hospital. Three pets are due to be released after surgery, so she begins preparing the invoices for the owners. Then the head of the hospital, Dr. Vicki Singler, interrupts her to ask why the new shipment of flea and tick medication hasn't arrived. "Oh," Julie answers, "I've been really busy, but I'll call that order in today, as soon as our patients are picked up."

"You haven't placed the order yet?" Dr. Singler says. "Julie, I asked you to do that last week, because flea season is starting. Couldn't you see it was a high priority?"

Julie feels herself sagging—the lack of sleep catching up with her—and she wonders why people are suddenly obsessed with "priorities."

What's Inside

Understanding Priorities

To set priorities means to decide which tasks need to be done in which order. If you're going to pursue the goals you set for yourself in Workshops 1 and 2, you need to establish priorities. Otherwise, minor chores and diversions will keep getting in the way of more important things.

The two main criteria for setting priorities are importance and urgency. It's crucial to realize that these are not the same thing.

Something that is *urgent* requires your immediate attention—it has to be done right away.

Something that is really *important*, in contrast, contributes to fulfilling your long-term goals.

Distinguishing importance from urgency is part of Julie's problem. It is very important to her to see Vanessa, and most of us would agree that friendships rate high on the scale of importance. But was it urgent that Julie see Vanessa on a particular night—so urgent that she should postpone the work for her class?

On the other hand, placing the order for medication didn't seem very urgent to Julie, though it was clearly important. So she spent her time instead on routine tasks. Clearly, her boss should have given her better guidance, but could Julie have done more on her own to establish priorities?

To help you begin thinking about importance and urgency, Activity 3.1 lists some typical tasks, most of which are probably familiar to you. The four categories used in the activity were developed by Stephen Covey and his coauthors in the book *First Things First*.

? Did you know

One of the most compelling examples of setting priorities is the practice of *triage*, a system used in emergency medicine. Derived from the French term for "sorting" or "sifting," triage means categorizing patients according to how much they need immediate treatment and how likely they are to benefit from it. Triage was developed during wartime, when priorities were literally a life-and-death matter.

> " The main thing is to keep the main thing the main thing. "
>
> — Stephen R. Covey, A. Roger Merrill, and Rebecca R. Merrill, *First Things First*

Urgent or Important?

Put a check mark in the column that identifies the level of importance and urgency of each item.

	A Urgent and Important	B Important but Not Urgent	C Urgent but Not Important	D Neither Urgent nor Important
1. Answering the phone at work	_____	_____	_____	_____
2. Helping a displeased customer	_____	_____	_____	_____
3. Loading paper in the printer	_____	_____	_____	_____
4. Stamping the mail	_____	_____	_____	_____
5. Going to lunch	_____	_____	_____	_____
6. Returning a phone call from your boss	_____	_____	_____	_____
7. Beginning the final draft of a report due in three days	_____	_____	_____	_____
8. Removing a spot from your shirt	_____	_____	_____	_____
9. Meeting with a co-worker about next month's plans	_____	_____	_____	_____
10. Attending a meeting about company benefits	_____	_____	_____	_____
11. Calling a friend to say "hello"	_____	_____	_____	_____
12. Attending to a crying baby	_____	_____	_____	_____
13. Ordering computer supplies for your department	_____	_____	_____	_____
14. Adding toner to the copier	_____	_____	_____	_____
15. Making plane reservations for tomorrow's last-minute trip	_____	_____	_____	_____
16. Making coffee	_____	_____	_____	_____
17. Reading your e-mail	_____	_____	_____	_____
18. Opening today's mail	_____	_____	_____	_____
19. Paying the phone bill that arrived today	_____	_____	_____	_____
20. Faxing a co-worker the agenda for next week's meeting	_____	_____	_____	_____

After completing this form, compare your answers with a classmate's or co-worker's. Where your answers differed, what different assumptions were you making?

Exploring the Four Categories

Let's look at the four categories in Activity 3.1 more closely to identify where the problems typically lie.

Category A: Urgent and Important. Everyone agrees that tasks in this category need to be done right away and done well. No argument—these are genuine priorities.

Category B: Important but Not Urgent. This category is where most of your long-term goals are located. It also includes things like taking care of your health, engaging in sufficient relaxation and recreation, developing your personal relationships, spending time with your family, and so on.

Category C: Urgent but Not Important. Many phone calls, some meetings, some lunch dates, a hairdresser's appointment—a lot of what we do falls into this category, demanding our attention right away without being truly important.

Category D: Neither Urgent nor Important. This was probably the category you assigned to item 16 in Activity 3.1, "making coffee." Other daily activities in this category might be: opening your junk mail; taking a trip to the store for ice cream; watching TV; listening to your latest music CD; chatting with co-workers about last weekend's football game.

Typically, the crunch comes from the fact that we spend a lot of time on activities in categories C and D. Category B tends to be neglected. Consequently, we make little progress toward our long-term goals, and we begin to feel frustrated and dissatisfied. Even when we divide our long-term goals into smaller steps, those steps remain in category B, and we may feel that we just don't have the time for them because of the crush of urgent matters.

Activity 3.2 will help you apply these ideas to your own life.

Urgent but unimportant

If a task seems urgent but not important, try asking yourself these questions about it:

✓ Who says this task is urgent?

✓ Are other people depending on me to do this?

✓ Does it have to be done now?

✓ Does it really have to be done at all?

✓ Could somebody else do it just as well, or at least acceptably?

✓ Can I combine this with another task and thereby save time?

Analyze Your Week

What Will You Be Doing?

List ten things you feel you will spend significant time on in the next week:

1. _____   6. _____

2. _____   7. _____

3. _____   8. _____

4. _____   9. _____

5. _____   10. _____

Applying the Four Categories

Now go back and analyze your next week's tasks in terms of the four categories, A through D. Be sure to use your personal evaluations of importance and urgency, not someone else's. For instance, jogging in the park may be a minor activity for some people; but if it's your primary means of exercise and recreation, then for you it's important.

In the form below, enter the tasks from your list (abbreviated if necessary) and use check marks to indicate the category for each item.

Task	A Urgent and Important	B Important but Not Urgent	C Urgent but Not Important	D Neither Urgent nor Important
1. _____	____	____	____	____
2. _____	____	____	____	____
3. _____	____	____	____	____
4. _____	____	____	____	____
5. _____	____	____	____	____
6. _____	____	____	____	____
7. _____	____	____	____	____
8. _____	____	____	____	____
9. _____	____	____	____	____
10. _____	____	____	____	____

Getting Tough with the Unimportant Stuff

By now you should have an idea what to do about the list you made in Activity 3.2.

♦ Begin by discarding everything from category D. If it's neither urgent nor important, why are you doing it?

♦ Then start cutting tasks out of category C. This chore is more difficult, but it's crucial if you want time for the important things in category B.

If you study your category C list carefully, you may find that some of the items have a *false urgency*. That is, your emotions have made them seem more urgent than they really are. Other items may indeed be urgent tasks, but not specifically for you—meaning that someone else perhaps could do them. If the phone rings at work while you're in the middle of an important job, for example, is it necessary for you to be the one who answers it?

ACTIVITY 3.3

Revising Your Priorities

As you've seen, the difficult part of revising your priorities is to cut down the time you spend on category C—the tasks that seem urgent but are not really important. Study each item you listed in column C in Activity 3.2, and come up with a plan for reducing the amount of time you spend on it. Use the hints in the box "Urgent but Unimportant" (p. 21) and any other strategies that you can devise.

Item from Category C   **My Plan for Reducing Time Spent on This Item**

1. _____   _____
                         _____

2. _____   _____
                         _____

3. _____   _____
                         _____

4. _____   _____
                         _____

5. _____   _____
                         _____

Testing Your Passion for Urgency

For each of the following statements, circle the answer that best describes you.

1.	When I'm rushing around, doing things under pressure, I feel good about myself— my competence, my usefulness, my intelligence.	Often	Sometimes	Never
2.	Even if tasks are relatively easy, I tend to let them go until they become urgent.	Often	Sometimes	Never
3.	I tend to do things in a hurry even when there's no particular need.	Often	Sometimes	Never
4.	When listening to other people on the phone, I tap my foot or drum my fingers because I'm impatient.	Often	Sometimes	Never
5.	I'm most energetic and lively when I have too many things to do.	Often	Sometimes	Never
6.	When I have an hour or two of extra personal time, I don't really know what to do with myself.	Often	Sometimes	Never
7.	Slow drivers really annoy me.	Often	Sometimes	Never
8.	People describe me as a workaholic.	Often	Sometimes	Never

The "Rush" of Urgency

Many people manage to weed out some of the category C tasks that gobble up their lives. But then they tend to use up the time they've saved by taking on, or even manufacturing, more tasks of the same type. As soon as they finish one frenzied project, they get involved in another—even though, in their most serious moments, they may realize that most of what they've been rushing to accomplish is unimportant.

You probably know some people of this type. Are they silly, self-destructive, or crazy? Not necessarily. Maybe they just love the "rush" or the "high" they get from being in crisis mode. Stephen Covey calls this an "addiction" to urgency.

We're all like that to some degree. Dealing with a crisis gives us a burst of adrenaline, and if we successfully negotiate the crisis, we feel a glow of satisfaction afterward. The problem arises when we get so hooked on living in crisis mode that most of the crises we're managing are really category C items—seemingly urgent but, in the long run, trivial. When the glow wears off, we feel gloomy and disillusioned.

If you answered "often" to more than one or two of the questions in Activity 3.4, you may need to deal with your passion for urgency. Get tough with the unimportant stuff! Set aside time each day for working on what's really important to you. Get serious about the plan that you developed in Activity 3.3.

If you work on it, you'll soon begin to find a "high" in making progress toward your goals—rather than in just surviving your crises.

For a more detailed evaluation of your feelings about urgency, try the Urgency Index Quiz by Stephen Covey and A. Roger Merrill, based on their book *First Things First*. At the time this book went to press, the quiz was on-line at the *USA Weekend* site. Go to

http://www.usaweekend.com/

and type the phrase *urgency quiz* in the search field.

Alternatively, to get an idea of how many other people have applied Covey's concepts of urgency and importance, do a Web search for relevant sites. Suggestion: Specify that the terms *Covey, first things first,* and *quadrant* must all appear. (Covey calls his four categories "quadrants.")

> " The central principle in time management is: *Spend your time doing those things you value or that help you achieve your goals.* "
>
> —Gillian Butler and Tony Hope, *Managing Your Mind*

WORKSHOP WRAP-UP

- Importance and urgency are not the same thing.
- Too often, the seemingly urgent keeps us from doing what is really important.
- Analyzing your weekly tasks on the basis of urgency and importance can help you redefine your priorities.
- You can make a plan for reducing the time you spend on urgent but unimportant activities.
- If you find you're deeply attracted to the "rush" you get from being in crisis mode, you need to get tough in making time for your more important goals.

Kevin's boss is normally as pleasant as the plump stuffed animals that are the company's main product. Today, though, Kevin finds a demanding message taped to the seat of his chair: "Kevin: That list of stores carrying the Wanda line—the list you were going to give me yesterday—I need it TOMORROW MORNING at the latest."

"Wanda" is Wanda B. Wombat, a washable marsupial who will make her debut next month. The company is doing an advance promotion, and Kevin's task has been to analyze sales records and compile a list of stores that have sold large numbers of similar products in the past. He's been delayed by the fact that he can't find the sales figures from the third quarter of last year.

Kevin knows he had those figures, but he has no clue where they are now.

Rather than ask for another printout, which would be embarrassing, he decides to search his work area again. The top of the desk is just as he left it—scattered with folders, stacks of loose papers, pencils, paper clips, a coffee cup, and an empty candy wrapper. Perhaps this was why his boss taped the note to the chair.

Though Kevin examines every paper on his desk—a process that takes over ten minutes— the sales figures don't emerge. In his filing drawer he finds another jumble. Half the folders are unlabeled, and they're in no particular order.

As Kevin is wasting valuable time in this way, his phone rings. "What happened to you at lunch yesterday?" his friend Eddie asks.

"Lunch yesterday? Nothing happened. Why?"

"We were getting together. Remember?"

Kevin slaps his forehead. "Hey, man, I'm sorry. I know I made a note to myself, but I forget where I put it."

What's Inside

In these pages, you will learn to:

Organization: A Tool You Can Use

We all get disorganized at times, especially when we're under pressure. But some of us, like Kevin, are chronically lacking in organization. Disorganized people cause themselves—not to mention their co-workers, friends, and family—a lot of extra grief. They misplace important materials. They waste time looking for things. They miss appointments or arrive late.

Think about people you know who, like Kevin, seem disorganized and inefficient. Do you get annoyed with them? Do you think of them as irresponsible? Do you worry about trusting them with a crucial job, afraid they'll lose track?

Now the key question: Could anyone ever think of *you* that way? Have there been at least a few times when you misplaced something essential or forgot to do something you'd promised?

There are no magic formulas for organizing your work or your life. But these two points may help you think about your organizational style:

1. *Organization is a tool you can use.* The word *organize* derives from an ancient Latin term meaning instrument or tool. The word's history helps make the point that organization is not a goal in itself but rather a tool that can help you accomplish *all* of your goals, from finishing today's work to achieving your life's dreams.

2. *Everyone can be better organized.* Maybe you don't suffer from Kevin's level of disorganization, but unless you're the world's only perfect person, you do sometimes misplace things and forget engagements.

Five top reasons for getting organized

1. Saving time—time you can use for activities you enjoy
2. Meeting deadlines
3. Improving your overall performance at work or in class
4. Reducing strain on your friends and on others who depend on you
5. Gaining control over your environment and your life

How Organized Are You?

Take this short quiz to evaluate your current organizational state. Check "Yes" or "No" after each statement.

		Yes	No
1.	I often feel rushed.	_____	_____
2.	I spend at least ten minutes each day looking for misplaced items such as my keys.	_____	_____
3.	I frequently start tasks at the last minute.	_____	_____
4.	I almost always feel that I have too much to do.	_____	_____
5.	I don't have enough room for all my stuff.	_____	_____
6.	At least once in the past two weeks, I missed a deadline or was late to meet someone.	_____	_____
7.	Often I handle the same papers or memos several times before I decide what to do about them.	_____	_____
8.	Before I start working on a project, it takes me a while to gather together what I need.	_____	_____
9.	Sometimes I lose track of due dates.	_____	_____
10.	Just looking at my desk makes me feel overwhelmed.	_____	_____

If you answered "yes" to more than one or two of these questions, you can definitely improve your level of organization.

Five unconvincing excuses for not organizing your desk

1. "I'm too busy to get organized."
2. "My chaos is a sign that I'm productive."
3. "If I file those papers, I'll never find them again!"
4. "The reason my space is disorganized is that they pile so much work on me."
5. "Neat people have uncreative minds."

Organizing Your Space: Neatness and Efficiency

To improve your personal organization, where should you start? How about the place you do most of your work—your desk and your workspace?

In some ways your desk reflects your personality. Maybe it's as neat as a pin. Maybe it's kind of untidy and artistic. There's an old saying that a messy desk is the sign of a messy mind. Often that's true. But "mess" to one person can be perfect order to another.

Peggy Gordon, who has run her own publishing business for nearly twenty years, tells the story of "the neatest employee I have ever had." This man was a model in terms of keeping his desk clean. Unfortunately, despite his tidiness, he often had trouble locating the papers he needed—he had tucked them away so compulsively that he couldn't find them. In his case, neatness did not equal efficiency.

What you want is a type of order that's best for you—a system that makes you efficient. For most of us, a moderate degree of neatness helps.

The relationship of neatness to efficiency can be illustrated with a simple example. Do you file your clean socks or hose in the same drawer as your underwear? Or do you keep them in a drawer with cough drops, shoelaces, and old ticket stubs? Nobody really cares. The system is up to you. But if you have no system—if your socks are so disorganized that you spend twenty minutes looking for two that match, so that you're late for work or class—people do care.

We can call this the Ready-to-Go Principle: The best organizational system is the one that makes you ready to go, minimizing the time you spend in preparation.

Here are some tips for applying the Ready-to-Go Principle to your own workspace:

♦ Keep things close to where they are used.
♦ Use the most convenient and easily reachable places for items you use the most.
♦ Use your desk drawers as organized filing areas; for instance:
  • Center drawer: pencils, pens, ruler, paper clips, organizational phone list
  • Side drawer: scissors, stationery, writing pads, memo forms, blank diskettes
  • Deep lower drawer: files for active projects
♦ Set up an area for older files or inactive projects, preferably away from your desk.
♦ Minimize personal items on your desk, such as family pictures and mementos. If they're really inspirational for you, fine; otherwise, they merely add to the clutter.
♦ At the end of the day, clear your desk of papers except for the project you will be working on tomorrow.
♦ At the end of the week, clean up your entire workspace, leaving out only what you'll need the next week.

If organizing your workspace seems like a daunting task, take it step by step. Break it down into smaller chunks. Set aside some time to work on it each day, and then do it!

Evaluating Your Workspace

Identifying the Necessaries

Make a list of ten tools, materials, or information sources you use regularly when you work. Paper, computer disks, stapler, list of phone numbers, stationery, dictionary, address book, project files—what do you need most often? Write them in the left-hand column below. Think about how accessible these necessities are for you. In the middle column, write down where you keep each item—or where you generally find it if you have to go searching for it. Then, in the right-hand column, make an honest estimate of the amount of time it typically takes to locate the item and get it ready to use.

Items Used Regularly	Where They Usually Are	Time Needed to Find
1.		
2.		
3.		
4.		
5.		
6.		
7.		
8.		
9.		
10.		

Making an Organizational Plan

Think about what you've learned. Are you wasting too much time fetching items you could have handy? Are you repeatedly searching your desk drawers for something you need every day? Use the form below to work out a plan for each type of inefficiency you have identified.

Type of Inefficiency	Solution
Always looking for diskettes	*Get a pack for my desk and keep it in top right-hand drawer*

Browse one or two on-line office-supply retailers to investigate the variety of desk organizers and accessories. You can find retailers by entering the phrase *office supplies* in a search engine, or you can try one of these:

The Keysan Catalog: **http://www.keysan.com/**
Office Depot: **http://www.officedepot.com/**
Quill: **http://www.quillcorp.com/**
Staples: **http://www.staples.com/**
Viking: **http://www.vikingop.com/**

What do you think of the desk organizers and related products you see advertised? Could you use any of them yourself—or could you create your own versions? What would be most helpful in getting yourself organized?

Coping with Information Overload

Our era has been labeled the Information Age. With researchers, government agencies, and businesses producing more and more data every day, there is more information available to us than ever before in human history. At the same time, advances in communication—television, radio, the World Wide Web, e-mail, cell phones—allow us to be bombarded with messages at virtually any time or place. Some people in large organizations receive so much e-mail that they can't possibly read it all and still do their jobs.

No wonder, then, that people often find themselves suffering from information overload. They are drowning in a sea of data. For that reason, being organized in dealing with information is more and more crucial for success, both in work and in life.

Did you know

Every year, on average, the National Archives and Records Administration—the agency charged with storing U.S. government records—receives about 1.5 million cubic feet of new records.

> Almost all new industries—and their jobs—are based on information skills.
>
> — Kevin Paul, *Study Smarter, Not Harder*

Efficient screening of information

How can you best cope with the information that pours in from every side? One useful approach is to get in the habit of screening every document that comes to you. *Screening* means scanning quickly to separate what you need to deal with from what you can safely ignore. You may find that many documents you receive are tossable—that is, they can go directly into the trash can or recycling bin. If documents are irrelevant to your purposes, screening lets you avoid wasting time on them.

In separating documents to keep from those to toss, here are some questions you can ask yourself:

♦ Will I use the information in this document?
♦ Will it help me do my work better?
♦ Is it still up-to-date and reliable?
♦ Should I refer it to someone else?
♦ If I toss it, could I replace it easily (for instance, by consulting a handy reference source)?
♦ Am I required to have it?

Efficient filing

Screening will help you get rid of many documents you don't need. For what you do have to keep, you should set up an efficient filing system. Here are several suggestions for filing:

1. Before you file a piece of paper, be sure that, next time you see it, you will know why you kept it. Write a note in the upper right corner, circle or highlight key points, flag important passages with sticky notes—do anything that will help you identify what's important about that piece of paper. You can use a similar technique with electronically stored documents: for instance, add a note to yourself at the beginning of the file or use the highlighting feature in your word processor.

2. Store like materials together. Usually this means putting all items for one project together in a file folder. Sometimes it may mean grouping papers according to the various roles you play: for instance, you might have one folder for items you need to discuss with your boss.

3. Label each file folder clearly with the name of the task or project. If you are keeping a mailing list for the Jones project, the tab on the folder should say something like "Jones Mailing List." Often it also helps to write the project name in large letters on the front of the folder, so that you can read it easily when the folder is sitting on your desk.

4. On the computer, use a similar system of folders—that is, set up separate electronic folders for different projects, each with a clear title.

5. Alphabetize all your folders by subject or topic.

6. If a folder becomes too big, split it into two or more folders. On the computer, use subfolders within larger folders: for instance, within an electronic folder called "Jones Project," you could have smaller ones called "Mailing List," "Correspondence," and so on.

> Apply the rule of *once past the desk*: Either deal with the task straight away, or decide when to deal with it and put it aside until that time.
>
> — Gillian Butler and Tony Hope, *Managing Your Mind*

Evaluating Your Filing System

Things I Could Toss

Are you saving documents you don't need? List some materials you have saved in your desk or filing cabinet that could be discarded without any appreciable loss. (If you use a computer regularly, think about what's stored on the hard drive.)

Old phone list from 1998 _____ _____

Outdated software manual _____ _____

_____ _____ _____

Products I Could Use to Help Myself Organize

Listed below are some common products that people use for organizing. Are you already using some of these? Could you make better use of them? For each item, decide whether you use it often, sometimes, or never and put a check in the appropriate box.

	Use Often	Use Sometimes	Never Use		Use Often	Use Sometimes	Never Use
Sticky notes	☐	☐	☐	Rolodex or similar card file	☐	☐	☐
Highlighters	☐	☐	☐	Electronic organizer	☐	☐	☐
Binder notebooks with dividers	☐	☐	☐	Calendar book or day planner	☐	☐	☐
Address book	☐	☐	☐	Calendar or planning software	☐	☐	☐

My Plan to Improve My Filing System

Using what you have learned, write out some ideas for improving your filing system.

Name my computer files more clearly and put them in folders under the project names. _____

_____

_____

_____

WORKSHOP WRAP-UP

- Getting organized can help you gain control of your life and save time for activities you enjoy.
- A good place to start your organizing is at your desk or workspace.
- The Information Age puts a premium on knowing what to toss, what to keep, and how to organize what you keep.

5 WORKSHOP

Anonda works in a large toy store. Recently promoted, she's been checking the computer records and the shelves to determine the current stock of every toy. This is her first time doing the monthly inventory check, and she wants it to be perfect.

Her main problem comes from continual interruptions to her work. Her best friend has just called to chat about another friend's upcoming wedding and the difficulty of finding a dress to wear. Anonda tried to cut the conversation short, but her friend talked for more than ten minutes. Meanwhile, in the past half hour, four e-mail messages have arrived, two of them from Anonda's boss, who always expects a quick answer. And her co-worker Torri keeps distracting her by stopping by every few minutes to chat.

Anonda answers her boss's e-mail message and goes out to the sales floor to check the stock of an electronic game. There the sales manager, Mark, intercepts her. "Anonda, we've got a crisis!" he says. "Those new action figures from the *Galactic Commandos V* movie are just flying off the shelves! Do we have more in the stockroom?"

"I don't know. My inventory check is stuck on aisle 4. Other things keep interfering."

"You have to help me search in back. We're desperate for Galactic Commandos!"

Shaking her head, Anonda follows Mark, worried that at this rate her work will never be completed.

What's Inside

In these pages, you will learn to:

> " Nothing is so dear and precious as time. "
>
> — François Rabelais

Managing Time

Anonda clearly has a problem. She has an important assignment, but friends, co-workers, even her boss seem to keep her from doing it. How can she cope with all these demands on her time?

We all have only 24 hours a day. That's 86,400 seconds. And each of those seconds, once used, can never be used again. That's why managing time is one of the most important skills you'll learn about in this book. Without adequate time, you can't complete your high-priority tasks or accomplish your ultimate goals. Without time for the things that are important to you, your life can be terribly frustrating.

This workshop and Workshop 6 focus on techniques to help you cope with time pressure. In the next few pages you'll find ideas for guarding your time from the people and circumstances that try to steal it. In Workshop 6 you'll learn ways to "make" time by using it more efficiently.

Controlling Interruptions

A major part of managing time is controlling interruptions. If you have a three-hour task to do, how likely is it that you'll be able to finish it without being interrupted? If you're like most people, you'll probably laugh at the question, because it seems that somebody or something is *always* interrupting you.

If you break down the interruptions into categories, though, you can identify ways to minimize them. Look at the following suggestions:

Interruption: The Telephone Ringing
POSSIBLE SOLUTIONS:

- Use caller ID to screen your calls.
- Use voice mail.
- Get someone else to take your calls while you're busy.
- Let people know which times are good for you to receive phone calls and which times are not good. Establish your own "telephone time."
- When you leave a message for someone to call you back, specify the time when you expect to be free.
- If all else fails, turn off the ringer.

Did you know

How many messages do you suppose a typical worker gets in a day? Think of phone calls, voice mail, e-mail, faxes, handwritten notes, and so on.

A few years ago, *USA Today* published the results of a survey taken among employees at Fortune 1000 companies. According to the survey, the average employee received 83 messages a day—not counting U.S. mail or courier services! With the increasing use of e-mail, that number is probably rising.

Interruption: People Dropping In
POSSIBLE SOLUTIONS:

- Find a more isolated place to work. Even an unconventional place can help—such as the cafeteria during off-hours.
- If you have your own door, close it.
- Position your desk away from the door.
- Remove chairs by your desk where people could sit down.
- Avoid eye contact when people pass by.
- Let people know when you don't want to be distracted. Set up a simple signal that tells people "I'm not available right now unless it's really important."
- When someone does stop by to visit, stand up. This helps you control the length of the interaction.
- In a conversation you want to terminate, use cues that lead toward an ending: for instance, "Before I get back to this project, is there anything else we need to go over now?"
- Say explicitly, "I'm wrapped up in something important right now. Can we talk later this afternoon?"

Interruption: E-mail
POSSIBLE SOLUTIONS:

- Set one or more specific times of the day for looking at your e-mail. The rest of the time, don't check it.
- If you receive a great deal of unnecessary e-mail, screen it before you read it. Just delete what you don't need to read.
- If you're routinely included in certain large-scale mailings that are irrelevant to you, see about having your name removed from those lists.
- Set up a second e-mail account for important messages. Give this address only to people whose messages you need to see right away.

Following these suggestions for controlling interruptions can help you get your work done on schedule. You'll feel less pressure, and some of the time you save can be devoted to pursuing your most important goals.

> Consider the postage stamp. It secures success through its ability to stick to one thing till it gets there.
>
> — Josh Billings

ACTIVITY 5.1

Recognizing the Intruders

Who or what are the major intruders on your time? On the lines below, list the five most common interruptions that keep you from concentrating on your work. Then write down one immediate and practical step you can take to shield yourself from each type of intrusion.

Time Intruder   **My Shield**

1. _____   _____

2. _____   _____

3. _____   _____

4. _____   _____

5. _____   _____

Quick Skills

GETTING CONNECTED

A second e-mail account may help you filter your mail. Your Internet service provider may allow you to set up multiple addresses—for example, one for business and one for personal use. If not, you still don't have to pay extra for a second account.

Companies like Hotmail offer Web-based e-mail without charge. There are also free e-mail services such as Juno that don't require you to have Web access. The number of options keeps expanding. Check out the "Free Email Address Directory" at this Web site:

http://www.emailaddresses.com/

Or simply enter the phrase *free e-mail* in a search engine and see what you turn up.

The Fine Art of Saying "No"

People are always asking for a piece of your time. Co-workers ask for your help with a project. Friends ask you to go to the movies. Maybe your sister calls to find out if you can watch her kids. Your supervisor assigns you another task. Too often, it seems, those little pieces of time you give out add up to the entire day. You end up not finishing important projects on schedule—and maybe having no time for the activities that are most important to you.

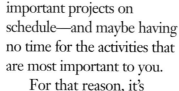

For that reason, it's important to know your own limitations. Don't take on more than you can manage—you'll only make yourself and everyone else unhappy with the results.

When someone tries to draw you beyond your limitations, you need to pronounce the two-letter word that Don Wetmore, president of The Productivity Institute, calls "one of the most powerful words in time management"—the word *no*.

Here are some general guidelines for saying "no" and making it stick:

- Be polite but firm.
- Explain your reasons.
- Thank the person for his or her interest in your participation. ("I'm flattered you asked me, but . . .")
- If you can, suggest other possibilities. ("Can you get Bill to help you?" "Amy is really better at this than I am." "How about if we do this next week when I'll have more time?")
- Remember, if you're really overloaded, you wouldn't be much help to the other person anyway.

But what if it's your boss who's piling too much on your plate? That situation may call for some special techniques:

- Ask your boss to rank the tasks you've been assigned in order of their priority.
- If two deadlines interfere with each other, point out the conflict.
- Negotiate your work load and your deadlines.
- Ask the boss if you can have help.
- If two different people with authority have assigned you conflicting tasks, ask them to talk to each other about the problem. Take yourself out of the middle.

ACTIVITY 5.2

Practice in Saying "No"

Imagine that you're working on Project A, a very important task that is due at the end of the week. Ned, a co-worker who is also a good friend, asks for your help with Project B. You know that Project B is important but not so urgent—and it's not directly your responsibility. How can you say "no" without damaging your relationship with Ned? Write three different responses you could use:

1. _____

_____

2. _____

_____

3. _____

_____

Delegation: Letting Others Do It

A final key to preserving your time is figuring out which of your tasks could be done by someone else. Effective time managers know how to *delegate* jobs to other people. Obviously this is easier for supervisors than for lower-ranking employees, but most of us have some occasions when we can get others to share the load. For instance, think about these common types of situations:

♦ Your company's sales manager is on a business trip. One day she phones the office to say she needs three boxes of samples packed up and expressed to her next stop. You're the one who happens to answer the phone, but you're very busy with another rush project. *Delegate!*

♦ You and five of your friends are planning to gather at Jim's house to watch a video on Friday night. On Thursday Jim calls you to say he's really sick with the flu and he'll have to cancel. He asks you to notify the others. But do you have to call each one? Maybe you could call Sarah, and she could call Jon, who could phone Tamika, and so on. *Delegate!*

♦ You're in charge of planning a small birthday party in the office for a fellow employee. You order the kind of cake she loves, and it has to be picked up at a bakery ten miles from your place. But one of your co-workers lives only five minutes from the bakery. *Delegate!*

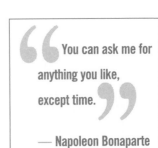

> You can ask me for anything you like, except time.
>
> — Napoleon Bonaparte

You may be reluctant to delegate work for a number of reasons. Maybe you're shy about approaching other people. Maybe you don't like to admit you're not Superman or Superwoman, able to handle 26 hours of work a day while leaping tall buildings. Maybe you think you'd be overstepping your authority if you tried to delegate. To deal with feelings like these, it helps to remind yourself that you don't do anyone a favor by getting so overburdened that you become ineffective.

The Big-I Theory

There may be one other reason you hesitate to delegate. Perhaps you believe in the Big-I Theory. The Big-I Theory states:

> "**I** am the only person in the world who can do this right!"

This is a very seductive way of thinking. We all subscribe to it at one time or another. And it's often partly true. There *is* nobody else who could do a job in exactly the way we think is right.

The problem is that our notion of the "right" way of doing a job is typically rather narrow. Usually someone else could do the task in a manner that other people, including the fussiest boss, would find acceptable. So we need to get over the Big-I way of thinking and admit that we're not indispensable. The reward—preserving our time for more important things—is worth the sacrifice of a little pride.

Rules for delegating effectively

When you do delegate, here are some suggestions for getting the best results:

- Whenever possible, delegate a whole job rather than just a fraction of it. This will make the other person more interested in the outcome.
- Pick a person with the skills and experience needed for the particular job.
- Explain the task fully, including the reasons for doing it.
- State the deadline clearly.
- Provide any necessary support.
- Monitor the progress regularly, but don't keep looking over the person's shoulder.
- Communicate your thanks when the job is done.

Did you know

The Executive Office of the President was created in 1939 by President Franklin D. Roosevelt "to protect the President's time" by "excluding any matter that can be settled elsewhere."

Tasks I Can Delegate

My Work Life

List some work tasks you might delegate and the people to whom you could delegate them. Also write a note to yourself about any special factors to consider: for instance, how and when to speak to the person; whether this individual will need training or practice; whether to consult your boss; and so forth.

Task	Person	Factors to Consider

My Personal Life

Now make a similar list for your personal life.

Task	Person	Factors to Consider

WORKSHOP WRAP-UP

- Managing time is a crucial part of self-management.
- By controlling interruptions, such as the telephone and unwanted visitors, you can make more productive use of your time and reduce the pressure on yourself.
- A two-letter word, "no," said politely but firmly, can work wonders in preserving your time.
- Often you can free blocks of time by delegating tasks and responsibilities to others.

At the bus stop Vijay fidgets, peering down the street for his bus. He's eager to get to the radio studio because his supervisor has given him a great assignment. The all-jazz station is planning a special for Valentine's Day, featuring romantic songs from the past half century. Vijay has been asked to comb the archives and come up with suggestions for the play list. Since he started work last year at an entry-level position, this is the first assignment he's received that will really call on his knowledge of jazz history and his enthusiasm for the music. The schedule is tight, though, because Valentine's Day is next week.

The bus still doesn't come. Vijay paces around and eventually pulls a paperback mystery from his jacket pocket. He reads a page and a half, finding it hard to concentrate. When the bus finally arrives, he locates a seat, reads a bit more, and then stares out the window, dreaming of the day when he'll have his own radio show.

At the radio station he rushes to his desk. There he finds the notes he made yesterday, plus some lists of the CDs, tapes, and records in the station's collection. But now that he's here, he doesn't know where to start. Chronologically with the 1950s or 1960s? Or with a particular artist? Eager to prove himself, he wants to do the job perfectly, and he worries about heading in the wrong direction. He gets a cup of coffee. He starts a new list of his own favorite classic love songs, then crosses out half of them. An hour later, he hasn't accomplished much except to raise his anxiety level, because now he's convinced he'll never finish on time.

What's Inside

In these pages, you will learn to:

♦ use "scraps" of time effectively ....p. 42

♦ reduce perfectionism ....p. 45

♦ combat indecisiveness........p. 46

♦ control time-wasting worries..............................p. 47

Scraps of Time

Like Vijay, we all seem to spend much of our time either waiting or rushing. And the more we wait, the more we have to rush to make up for the lost time.

Think of the various ways you spend time waiting:

- At bus or train stops
- In doctors' and dentists' offices
- In line at stores, banks, post offices, movie theaters, concerts
- On hold during phone calls
- At restaurants
- In a barber shop or hair salon

With a bit of thought, you could probably add several more items to that list. Each instance of waiting might take only a few minutes, but all together those little scraps of time add up to a significant amount.

Besides waiting, we often have to do tasks that are essentially no-brainers: driving or riding to work, washing the dishes, folding laundry, making photocopies, paying bills, stamping envelopes. During these tasks our minds aren't really engaged, so that, too, is a kind of dead time.

One key to good time management is realizing that these scraps of time can be used effectively.

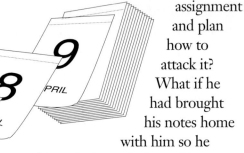

What if, instead of reading a mystery novel, Vijay had used his time at the bus stop and on the bus to concentrate on his assignment and plan how to attack it? What if he had brought his notes home with him so he could study them during odd moments? By using his miscellaneous time in such ways, he might have had a head start before he reached his desk. Even though time can't be manufactured, he would have "made" more time for himself.

? Did you know

Although our "scraps" of time may be impossible to measure precisely, these estimates have been published:

♦ *Waiting:* Each American spends about 175 hours a year in various kinds of waiting.

♦ *Commuting:* Americans who drive to work spend an average of over 45 minutes each day en route. For people who use public transportation, a round trip takes about an hour and a half.

Here are a few suggestions for saving time by filling up those precious minutes you spend waiting or engaged in routine tasks:

- Carry a notebook with you at all times so you can jot down ideas that occur to you about a current project or an upcoming task.
- Always have some useful reading with you, such as a report or magazine article you need to read.
- On your car stereo, listen to informational tapes or CDs while you're driving. Do the same with a portable cassette or CD player while you're walking, riding, or exercising.
- On a plane or train trip, make the travel time into work time by reading, doing paperwork, writing notes or letters.
- While doing routine tasks such as photocopying, do something with your brain as well: plan your next job, for instance.
- While watching TV, do something with your hands: fold that laundry, stamp those outgoing letters.
- If you have to wait for your computer to download a file, do something else in the meantime: write a note, pay a bill, locate the materials you need for your next step.
- If you're kept on hold on the phone, sort your mail or scan the next item you need to read.

> ❝ Lost time is never found again. ❞
>
> —Benjamin Franklin

GETTING CONNECTED

Browse on-line for audiobooks on a subject you'd like to learn about—maybe one related to your career plans. The large on-line booksellers often list audiobooks as a separate subject category. Check these booksellers, for instance:

http://www.amazon.com/
http://www.bn.com/

There are also on-line retailers that specialize in audiobooks, such as these:

http://www.audiobooks.com/
http://www.audiobooksonline.com/
http://www.spoken-word.com/

By searching for the term *audiobooks,* you can find other sites as well.

On the basis of what you learn on-line, decide whether renting or purchasing some audiobooks would be a good way to reclaim some of the time you lose in waiting, traveling, or doing routine chores.

ACTIVITY 6.1

Locating Your Scraps of Time

With what you've read so far, you should be able to identify the common occasions when you lose scraps of time. Use the lines below to name some of your personal time-wasters and work out a plan for making better use of the precious minutes. Remember, a scrap of time can be a truly small amount—any time during which you could be doing something useful.

Where I Waste Time	Amount of Time Lost	My Plan for Using the Time Productively
1. _____	_____	_____
2. _____	_____	_____
3. _____	_____	_____
4. _____	_____	_____
5. _____	_____	_____

Personality-Based Time Wasters

In the scenario at the beginning of this workshop, you may have noticed that Vijay's time problems related in some ways to his personality. He wanted so much to do his job perfectly that he wasted time deciding what to do first and worrying about his situation. For many people, these characteristics—perfectionism, indecisiveness, and a tendency to worry— are frequent time thieves. Often they're ingrained in our personalities, so we have to make a special effort to conquer them. The rest of this workshop will focus on ways to fight these personality-based time wasters.

? Did you know

If you save just seven minutes a day, by the end of a year you'll have gained more than a typical workweek of time!

Perfectionism

Do you sometimes find yourself checking a job three times to make sure it's exactly right? Do you have trouble making time for all your tasks because you spend so many hours on one? Are you known for being a fanatic about small details? Do you notice that other people seem to accomplish the same job in less time and get full credit for it, even though their work may not be as absolutely spotless as yours?

If you answered "yes" to any of these questions, you may be a perfectionist. As the saying goes, "Nobody's perfect," but many of us try too hard to be. Perfectionism involves spending so much time trying to do tasks perfectly that the overall quality of your work declines.

If this characteristic is one of your own time thieves, try to keep it under control. The answer is not to do a sloppy job, of course, but to apportion your time wisely, give each task just the effort it requires, and know when enough is enough. Ask yourself questions like these:

♦ Am I spending time on minor details that are irrelevant?
♦ Am I getting behind in the rest of my work because of unnecessary time spent on this task?
♦ Does the law of diminishing returns apply here—that is, am I getting less and less out of each additional unit of time I spend?

? Did you know

Time pressures on the average family are so great that, according to a survey by a University of Detroit researcher, parents and children spend only $14^1/_2$ minutes a day talking to each other.

ACTIVITY 6.2

Am I Too Much of a Perfectionist?

Think about what you've learned about perfectionism. Do you ever behave like a perfectionist? If so, use the lines below to identify some ways you could save time by being a little less worried about absolute perfection. List some tasks that you try to do perfectly, and then write down a "less perfect" method that would still be completely acceptable for you and everyone else concerned.

At work

Task	My "Less Perfect" (But Still High-Quality) Approach
1.	
2.	
3.	
4.	
5.	

At home

Task	My "Less Perfect" (But Still High-Quality) Approach
1.	
2.	
3.	
4.	
5.	

Indecisiveness

Perfectionism's frequent companion is indecisiveness. If you're too concerned that the outcome be perfect, too terrified of making a mistake, it's hard to make decisions. You keep searching for the one absolutely best choice when in reality there are many workable choices.

In Workshop 7 we'll look at procrastination, which is the habit of putting things off till a later time. Here, the point is simply that being indecisive can be a waste of time in itself. Precious minutes or even hours fly by while you're debating what to do.

To make any decision effectively, you need to gather the appropriate information, consider the alternatives, weigh the advantages and disadvantages of each choice, and analyze how they fit your priorities. Then you're ready to make your decision, so go ahead and make it! Postponing it usually won't accomplish anything.

> **One always has time enough, if one will apply it well.**
>
> — Johann Wolfgang von Goethe

Am I Indecisive?

Do a mental review of your past week. Were there any instances when you wasted time by being indecisive—by not making a decision and going ahead with it? If so, list those occasions, then try to figure out the reason for your indecisiveness in each case.

Type of Indecision	Reason I Was Indecisive
1.	
2.	
3.	
4.	
5.	

Worrying

Some people seem to sail through life without a care in the world. Some people are constantly biting their fingernails. In between are most of us who, though not constant worriers, do get held up by anxieties at crucial moments.

When you have a big job or critical decision ahead, worry can actually slow you down. It can contribute to indecisiveness or perfectionism. It can make you fret so much that your concentration is ruined.

Often the best solution to time-stealing worries is simply to immerse yourself in the job. For instance, if you're worried about preparing a big report for your boss, just start doing it. Begin to collect the information you need and make some notes. Once you're actively working on the project, your worries will be pushed to the back of your mind, and your progress will help ease your remaining doubts.

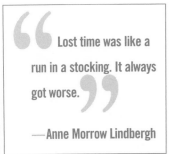

> Lost time was like a run in a stocking. It always got worse.
>
> —Anne Morrow Lindbergh

If you need a more structured approach, consider the "worry decision tree" recommended by psychologist Gillian Butler and psychiatrist Tony Hope in their book *Managing Your Mind*. The "tree" consists of a series of three questions that you pose to yourself:

- Ask yourself what you are worrying about. Make the object of your worry clear to yourself.
- Ask yourself whether you can do something about the problem that's worrying you. If you can't do anything about it, shove the worries aside and get on with your life; what's going to happen is going to happen. But if you *can* do something about it, decide exactly what to do and make a plan for action.
- If you've decided there is something you can do, ask yourself whether it can be done at this very moment. If so, do it. If not, decide when you'll do it and get on with something else.

ACTIVITY 6.4

Am I a Worrywart?

Identifying My Worries

Review your past week. Have you had any worries, either major or minor, that occupied your time? If so, list them here:

1. _____
2. _____
3. _____
4. _____
5. _____

Forming an Antiworry Plan

Now make a plan for conquering each of your time-gobbling worries. Figure out what you can do about the problem and when you can do it.

Worry	What I Can Do	When I Can Do It
1. _____	_____	_____
2. _____	_____	_____
3. _____	_____	_____
4. _____	_____	_____
5. _____	_____	_____

WORKSHOP WRAP-UP

- By making good use of the scraps of time you spend waiting or doing routine tasks, you can "make" time for more important matters.

- If you have a tendency toward perfectionism, you may be spending too much time polishing up little details that no one else cares about.

- Indecisiveness, often tied to perfectionism, can also waste significant amounts of your time.

- Worrying can steal your time by making you indecisive or keeping you from concentrating. Often you can handle worry by confronting the problem that's bothering you and making a plan for dealing with it.

It's Sunday evening, and Tai's class assignment is due tomorrow at 6:00 P.M. Currently Tai is an administrative assistant in the Communications Department of an engineering firm. To improve her skills, she's been taking an evening course in business writing.

The assignment is to write an interview article. Three weeks ago, when the instructor explained the assignment, Tai decided to interview Melissa Tharp of her company's research and development branch about future trends in the industry. Maybe, she thought, if she did a really great article, her boss might publish it in the company's newsletter.

She felt shy, though, about approaching Ms. Tharp, and she put off asking for an interview until a few days ago. Luckily Ms. Tharp agreed to talk with her. Since they are both busy during weekdays, they decided to do the interview by phone sometime over the weekend.

Tai knew she ought to plan some questions to ask. She was going to do it Friday night, but she became engrossed in a TV show. On Saturday, laundry and other housework took up her time. That night, when she tried to focus on interview questions, she didn't know where to begin. Worried about doing a poor job, she figured she needed to be in exactly the right frame of mind to plan the interview properly.

Sunday morning there was the newspaper to read, and the afternoon was so beautiful she took her dog for a walk in the park.

Now it's 8:00 Sunday night, and Tai is feverishly scribbling questions. At last she's energized, and she feels a kind of rush as she dials Ms. Tharp's home number.

The phone rings and rings and rings.

What's Inside

In these pages, you will learn to:

Tomorrow, Tomorrow, I'll Get It Done Tomorrow

Tai, as you can see, does a good job of *procrastinating*, which means putting off a task until a later time. With this technique, she manages to turn a three-week assignment into a last-minute crisis. Do you think it's just this particular task she postpones, or is it likely she procrastinates at other times as well?

We all procrastinate in any number of small ways. Maybe you've been promising yourself for years that you'll clean out the top drawer of your dresser or that you'll organize your collection of snapshots. If the task you're postponing is minor, there's no harm in letting it slide. Maybe you're actually using your time for more important things.

The problem comes, of course, when the task you put off is really significant. As long as only your low-priority items are being postponed, you're probably okay. But when it's high-priority matters that get short shrift because you left them till the last minute, you're in trouble. You'll likely have extra anxiety and stress because of your delay, and often your performance will suffer as well.

> Procrastination is the art of keeping up with yesterday.
>
> —Don Marquis

Words for the wise—and not so wise

♦ In the eighteenth century, Ben Franklin published the famous aphorism, "Never leave that till tomorrow which you can do today."

♦ In the nineteenth century, William Brighty Rands retorted (tongue in cheek), "Never do today what you can put off till tomorrow."

♦ Which best describes your attitude?

This doesn't apply just to work habits. Procrastination can affect the most personal aspects of your life. Often people postpone discussing family problems because it's too difficult or embarrassing. Unfortunately, the frequent result of ignoring minor problems is that they grow to be major ones.

For a small percentage of people, procrastination becomes such a serious obstacle that it requires treatment by medical specialists. Many entire books have been written about the causes, effects, and treatment of procrastination, and research studies link it to depression, chronic anxiety, and low self-esteem.

To see if you have difficulty because of procrastination, try the following activity.

Measure Your Procrastination Tendencies

For each item, circle the answer that best represents you.

1.	I convince myself that seeing a movie or watching TV will help me finish a project because I'll feel more relaxed afterward.	Often	Sometimes	Never
2.	I put off chores when I'm not in the mood for them or when I'm just not ready.	Often	Sometimes	Never
3.	I ignore tasks I don't want to do, hoping somehow I'll get out of doing them.	Often	Sometimes	Never
4.	I make a show of working—piling my desk with the materials, carrying my books around, and so on—without actually doing much.	Often	Sometimes	Never
5.	I concentrate on a pleasant or neutral task instead of finishing a more important job I don't like.	Often	Sometimes	Never
6.	I let myself have minor diversions that, as it turns out, eat up most of my work time.	Often	Sometimes	Never
7.	I manage to believe there's plenty of time left even when there isn't.	Often	Sometimes	Never
8.	With big tasks I'm a slow starter because I don't know how to begin.	Often	Sometimes	Never
9.	I have to rush to finish a project on time because I didn't get started soon enough.	Often	Sometimes	Never
10.	Because I have an unfair amount of work to do, I let some of it slide.	Often	Sometimes	Never

If you answered "often" to more than one or two of these questions, you may need to face up to your procrastinating tendencies. Read the following sections for some ideas.

Reasons for Procrastination

People procrastinate for a wide variety of reasons. One frequent and very natural reason is that the task is unpleasant. Maybe you hate the dentist's office, so you put off having your teeth cleaned. Perhaps you've been asked to make forty copies of a report, collate them, and staple them, and you avoid the task as long as you can because it seems so deadly dull.

Often, though, there are deeper psychological causes of procrastination. Here are some of the reasons that psychologists have identified:

- *Fear of failure (performance anxiety):* If the task is hard, you may worry that other people won't like the way you did it. Or you may be concerned about being a failure in your own eyes, especially if you're a perfectionist. In either case, your anxiety can persuade you to dodge the task as long as possible.
- *Fear of the unknown:* If you're faced with a job you've never done before, you may have a kind of formless fear about what will happen when you try it.
- *Fear of success:* Who, you may ask, would be afraid of succeeding? Well, someone who wants to avoid increased responsibility, for instance. Or someone who dreads the limelight. Or someone who's afraid others will be jealous.

- *Rebelliousness or revenge:* Say you're facing a task assigned to you by another person. You don't like that person, or you don't like being forced to do such things, or you think the task is irrelevant, stupid, or unfair. In any of these cases, you may conduct a little internal rebellion by seeking to avoid the task. Moreover, if the person is counting on you, your avoidance becomes a form of revenge.

Urgency addiction: As you learned in Workshop 3, there's a certain "high" associated with urgency. When you start rushing to complete a task, going all out, the adrenaline flows and you feel intensely alive. Some people procrastinate in part because they like this feeling.

Self-handicapping: In horse racing a handicap is the weight a horse is assigned to carry. Sometimes people handicap themselves by adding difficulty to a task, making it less possible that they'll accomplish the job successfully. Procrastination can be one means of self-handicapping. Why would anyone do this? The psychological possibilities are complex, but often the goal of self-handicapping is to have a built-in excuse for failure. "Oh, I didn't do too well on that project, but of course I was rushed, so I know it wasn't my best job. I could actually do it magnificently under better circumstances."

These psychological reactions can exist in many different combinations. Any serious instance of procrastination may involve more than one of them.

Finally, there's one other reason for procrastination that deserves mention. Some people believe that, if they put off doing their work long enough, somebody else will do it, or magically the need for it will disappear. Occasionally this assumption proves true, but not often.

ACTIVITY 7.2

Identifying Your Reasons for Procrastinating

Do any of the reasons for procrastination described in the preceding section sound familiar to you? Have you ever, for instance, postponed an assignment because of fear of failure, or perhaps out of rebellion because you thought what you were being asked to do was unfair? Think seriously about your usual reasons for procrastinating and list them on the lines below, along with an example of each.

Reason	An Instance When I Procrastinated for This Reason
1. _____	_____
2. _____	_____
3. _____	_____
4. _____	_____
5. _____	_____

Fighting Procrastination

The first step in overcoming procrastination is to confess that you're doing it. Be honest; don't delude yourself. Face up to the negative consequences, too. Make yourself admit the ways your life could have been better if you had worked at things rather than putting them off.

After you've done that much, you can attack the problem with these further steps:

Changing your behavior

- If you're a habitual procrastinator, begin your reform with a single task or a single area of your life. Don't try to tackle all your procrastination problems at once.
- Divide large tasks into smaller components.
- Set aside specific blocks of time to work on the small component tasks. Schedule a beginning time and an end. That way, you'll know when you have to start, but you'll also have promised yourself a specific time to stop, and the task won't seem too overwhelming.
- When possible, do a little work on your small tasks during your "scrap" moments of time, as described in Workshop 6.

- Write reminders to yourself and put them where you can't help but see them—for instance, on your telephone or your computer monitor.
- Remove yourself as far as possible from tempting distractions, such as TV, radio, and the telephone.
- Plan short breaks in your work—say, ten minutes each hour. Do something pleasant for that short time and congratulate yourself on how much you've accomplished.
- After each chunk of the task is completed, reward yourself: a healthy snack, a movie, music, whatever you enjoy. If you're at the office and can't get your reward immediately, promise it to yourself for the earliest available time, such as that very night. For large chunks of the task, plan a big reward— and write it on your calendar so you can look forward to it.

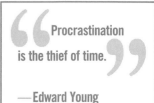

> Procrastination is the thief of time.
>
> —Edward Young

Getting support from others

However you decide to battle procrastination, it can be helpful to enlist the support of others. For instance, let your friends in on your plan so they can pat you on the back when you stick to it. If you're taking courses, you may want to arrange for a study partner. Similarly, at your job, you may be able to find a "task partner"—someone of a similar age and position with whom you can cooperate for mutual improvement. You can monitor each other's progress and offer encouragement (or chocolate bars) at appropriate times.

Changing your thinking

Negative feelings and unproductive behavior often stem from negative thoughts. To overcome such thoughts, you can modify your "self-talk." *Self-talk* consists of the things we say to ourselves privately, often almost automatically.

For instance, when you get a big assignment, you may tend to mutter, "I can't possibly do this. I already have too much work." Or "I don't know how to do this, I'll mess it up." Or "This isn't fair—why dump this job on me?" With any such response, you're already set up for procrastination and other types of self-defeating behavior.

In such cases, you can help yourself by pinpointing that negative thought. Write it down and study it. Then, if it's wrong (as most negative thoughts tend to be), write down the reasons why it's untrue.

For example:

Negative Thought
"I don't know how to do this, so I'm bound to make a mistake."

Possible Response
"I've frequently done a good job even on new kinds of tasks. And I do have some relevant experience. Besides, I can ask for help with the parts I'm unsure about. And if I do make a mistake, so what? Nobody's perfect."

GETTING CONNECTED

For more on self-talk, check out "The Hot 100" list of frequently used examples of negative self-talk:

http://www.selftalk.com/whatis/hot100.htm

Also, by entering the phrase *negative self-talk* or *positive self-talk* in a search engine, you can get a sense of how important the concept has become in the fields of psychology and self-help.

Worksheet 7: Overcoming Procrastination

Breaking the Habit of Procrastination

Here are some exercises that will get you started on the path to reducing your procrastination.

Facing the Consequences

On the lines below, list some consequences you have suffered because of procrastination at work, at school, or in your personal life. Have you missed getting a raise because your projects tend to be late? Were your school grades lower than they could have been because you often postponed your studying?

Situation   **Consequences**

_____   _____

_____   _____

_____   _____

_____   _____

Countering Your Best Excuses

Think about your self-talk. List the best excuses you give yourself for procrastinating and then, beside each one, list something else more positive that you could say to yourself instead.

My Excuse   **My Positive Replacement Thought**

1._____   _____

2._____   _____

3._____   _____

4._____   _____

5._____   _____

Taking Baby Steps

As you've learned earlier in this book, a key to self-management is breaking down large, intimidating tasks into smaller components that you can handle more easily. You don't need to be ashamed if your first steps are "baby steps." Isn't that true of everybody?

On the lines below, list just one big task (preferably an important task) that you've been postponing. Then write down some smaller steps that you can take to move toward completing it.

Big Task I've Been Postponing   **Small Steps I Can Take to Accomplish It**

_____   _____

                                 _____

                                 _____

                                 _____

WORKSHOP WRAP-UP

- Procrastination is putting things off till a later time.
- Though we all procrastinate sometimes, it becomes a problem when it's habitual or when we postpone an important task.
- Procrastination stems from many causes, including fear of failure, rebelliousness, and self-handicapping.
- We can conquer procrastination by modifying our behavior and our negative thinking.

8 WORKSHOP

Carlos's boss, Ms. Polonski, wants to upgrade the appointment-planning software that the company's sales reps use on their laptop computers. She asks him to survey the available software products and give her a recommendation, along with an estimate of the total price. The deadline is in two weeks.

Carlos immediately checks all the major suppliers on the Internet, scans the blurbs about their products, reads some on-line reviews, and downloads trial versions of three different programs. All this in the first afternoon—a quick start! Over the next few days, whenever he has a few moments free, he tries out the programs and makes a list of pros and cons for each one.

By the next week, he decides which product he will recommend. He calls the manufacturer to determine the price for a corporate sale. "How many copies?" he is asked. Carlos doesn't know the exact number, and the manufacturer isn't willing to quote until he does.

Carlos goes to Pauline Bichette in Sales to ask how many reps are using laptops. "Which kind?" she responds. It turns out the reps have a wide range of computers. When Carlos mentions the software he's evaluating, Pauline says she's not sure the older machines could run it.

"Uh-oh," Carlos says. "Can you give me a list of exactly what they've got, how many of each kind of machine, and so on?"

"Not off the top of my head," Pauline grumbles. "Check with me next week."

When Carlos returns to his desk, it occurs to him that his efforts may have been wasted. Maybe the software he's been examining isn't the right type at all. Besides, it now looks like he'll miss the deadline Ms. Polonski gave him.

What's Inside

In these pages, you will learn to:

Why Plan?

What an irony for Carlos! His mistake in evaluating the new appointment-planning software was his own lack of planning.

That mistake was especially noticeable because he did many other things right—he didn't procrastinate, he used his spare time wisely, and he organized his notes in an effective fashion.

His story illustrates some of the problems that result from lack of planning:

♦ Waste of effort
♦ Waste of time
♦ Missed deadlines
♦ Frustration
♦ Ineffective coordination among the various people involved

Sometimes our failures to plan come from eagerness to get started. Planning, after all, is often boring compared with the job itself, so it's tempting to jump in and begin the work. Other reasons for failing to plan include these:

♦ Not recognizing the importance of planning
♦ Not understanding the complexity of the job
♦ Feeling that there isn't enough time to spend on planning
♦ Laziness
♦ Reluctance to get fully engaged in the task or to take responsibility for it

The basis of planning is simply thinking ahead. Would you take a job or enroll in a school without thinking ahead? Would you get married without thinking ahead? If not, then it makes sense to think ahead when you take on other important projects.

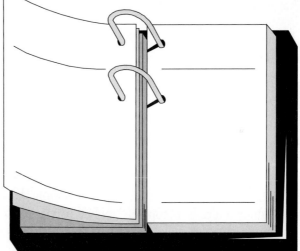

Evaluate Your Planning Habits

For each statement below, circle the answer that best applies to you.

1. When faced with a significant task, I make a point of planning how to approach it.	Often	Sometimes	Never
2. I gather information carefully before I start a job.	Often	Sometimes	Never
3. I write out my plans on paper or on my computer.	Often	Sometimes	Never
4. In my planning, I decide how to involve other people—for instance, I figure out whom to consult and which parts of the task I can delegate.	Often	Sometimes	Never
5. I approach a large task by dividing it into small steps.	Often	Sometimes	Never
6. Before rushing into things, I think about what I need to do first.	Often	Sometimes	Never
7. When someone gives me a big deadline, I establish my own intermediate deadlines for separate parts of the task.	Often	Sometimes	Never
8. If an unforeseen event interrupts my plan, I can adjust without losing much time.	Often	Sometimes	Never
9. My major projects are finished on time.	Often	Sometimes	Never
10. My planning allows me free time for the things I really like to do.	Often	Sometimes	Never

How many times did you answer "sometimes" or "never"? Do you think you're an effective planner?

Top Ten Tips for Effective Planning

Although each task is different, there are some general guidelines that can help you become an effective planner. Here is a "top ten" list of tips:

1. *Make time for planning.* Planning uses time in the beginning, but it saves time overall. Don't get so caught up in the rush of work that you forget to put aside time for planning.

2. *If a task requires research, do it early.* Research in this sense means any gathering of information—from books, reports, magazines, the Internet, or other people. If you put off learning what you need to know, you may start off on the wrong track.

3. *Identify the possible routes to your goal and select the best one.* You can use brainstorming to identify your options (see Workshop 1). Also make use of all your other resources, such as the knowledge of co-workers. Then evaluate the different alternatives and make the best choice.

4. *Divide the task into small steps.* This is advice you've heard several times in this book. As the age-old maxim puts it, "Divide and conquer."

5. *Understand the order of steps: put first things first.* Doing things in the right order is often a key to doing them right. Figure out which stages of the project are likely to produce results or information that will modify the way you approach the other stages.

6. *Decide whether any of the steps can be delegated and to whom.* One great benefit of planning is that you may identify ways that other people can do some of the work!

7. *Work backward from the deadline; set intermediate deadlines.* Planning works best when you do it backward. That isn't as odd as it sounds. Say you've identified steps A, B, C, and D that will lead you to goal E. Working back from the deadline for E, ask yourself when D needs to be finished. Then, moving backward from D, schedule the completion of step C, and so on.

8. *Put your plan in writing.* Writing your plan down helps you identify any gaps or problems. It also helps you remember what you're doing!

9. *Periodically evaluate your plan's progress and make revisions as needed.* Even the best planners can't foresee everything that may happen along the way. Schedule certain points at which you'll review your progress and decide whether to modify the plan.

10. *Maintain flexibility.* The best plans include fudge factors. They may allow a bit of extra time so that, if you fall behind on one or two steps, you can catch up. Or they may include alternatives for key stages or elements. For instance, your plan may indicate that if the final sales figures are ready in time for your report, you'll include them; if they're not ready, you'll use estimates that you know will be available.

> **It is a bad plan that admits of no modification.**
>
> —Publius Syrus

Did you know

In a survey of American workers by Day-Timers, 50% admitted they did not usually make plans for achieving their goals.

Planning a Project

Think about a major project you have to accomplish in the next few weeks. Describe that project here and indicate its deadline:

Project   **Deadline**

_____   _____

Now use the following steps to help plan your approach.

Divide and Conquer

Break your project down into smaller components and list them:

_____   _____   _____

_____   _____   _____

_____   _____   _____

First Things First

Now go back and put the component steps in the order in which they ought logically to be done. You can do this by writing a letter next to each item: (A) for the first, (B) for the second, and so on.

Intermediate Deadlines

Now work out a reasonable deadline for each of the separate steps you've identified. Begin with the last step and work backward to the present time.

	Step	**Deadline**
(Last step)	_____	_____
	_____	_____
	_____	_____
	_____	_____
	_____	_____
	_____	_____
	B	_____
(First step)	A	_____

All right, you have your project planned. Now do it!

GETTING CONNECTED

Because planning is such a basic need, software and electronics companies have been quick to produce computerized aids, ranging from software programs to hand-held electronic organizers. There are even Web sites that offer personalized planning help. The generic term *PIM*, which stands for "personal information manager," is often used to refer to all these possibilities.

Check out a few PIMs on-line. Enter the term *PIM* (in all capitals) in a search engine, or use a directory such as Yahoo! (**http://www.yahoo.com/**). You'll find listings of various PIM products. Or go to an on-line computer magazine and use the same search term to find reviews. One fairly nontechnical magazine is *FamilyPC* (**http://www.zdnet.com/familypc/**).

Time Estimates

In Activity 8.2 you may have found that the most difficult part was the last one. To set deadlines for the various steps of a project, you need to decide how much time to allow for each step, and that is sometimes hard to do.

On some occasions in your life, a project may involve several steps that are new to you. It may feel almost like you've been asked to explore Mars. In that case, even if you divide the job into components, how can you possibly estimate the time you'll need for each step?

Here are a few suggestions:

♦ Engage in analogical thinking. That is, think of something else you've done before that is roughly similar (analogous) to the task in question. Even if the parallel isn't exact, you'll get some idea of the amount of time you'll need.

♦ Consult other people who have done this task or a similar one. Ask them how long they would need, and then allow extra time because of your inexperience.

♦ Do a quick check for other sources that may offer guidance—books, tapes, Internet sites, and so on.

♦ Try a short test. By seeing how far you get in, say, one hour, you may help yourself judge how long the entire task may take.

As you gain experience, you'll become better and better at estimating time. It's a skill that you can acquire—if you work at it.

> " Nine-tenths of wisdom consists in being wise in time. "
>
> —Theodore Roosevelt

ACTIVITY 8.3

Estimating Time

For practice in estimating time, write in the amount of time you think you would need for each of the activities listed below:

Activity	Estimated Time
1. Cleaning up your workspace at the end of the week	_____
2. Shopping for a week's groceries	_____
3. Finding a book about time management at the library	_____
(include your time getting to and from the library)	_____
4. Copying 30 pages (include your time to and from the copier)	_____
5. Updating your resume and printing a new copy	_____
6. Taking your car to a garage for service and explaining what you want to have done	_____
7. Describing your job to a new employee	_____
8. Typing and printing a one-paragraph letter and preparing it for mailing	_____
9. Reading a four-page, double-spaced report	_____
10. Writing a four-page, double-spaced report	_____

The next time you do any of these tasks, clock your actual time and compare it with your estimate. How accurate were you?

WORKSHOP WRAP-UP

- Planning can save you effort and time and help you meet your deadlines.
- Guidelines for effective planning include dividing a big task into small steps, putting the steps in the right order, and setting a deadline for each.
- Good planning depends on estimating how much time each task will take. Estimating time is a skill you can improve by working at it.

Angela works for an on-line store that sells books, CDs, and tapes through a Web site. Business is booming, and Angela's job involves helping to coordinate special promotions.

Angela considers herself an organized and productive person. She keeps a mental list of everything she needs to do at work and at home. She keeps her desk neat, her papers and computer files in order, and her projects on schedule— except on the few occasions when she happens to forget something. Unfortunately, one of those occasions was yesterday.

In connection with a new album released by a well-known rock group, the store is offering a limited-edition collection of the group's greatest hits. A customer who buys the new album gets a discount on the collection. One of Angela's tasks for yesterday was to gather up all the necessary information for this promotion and forward it to the people who set up the "Today's Features" section of the home page.

She saved her boss's e-mail memo outlining the task, and she meant to get started yesterday morning, but in the midst of umpteen other jobs she simply forgot. In the afternoon, when her boss asked about it, she made an excuse and started scrambling. She did manage to pull the information together by 4:00. As a result of being rushed and exhausted, though, she forgot to include one crucial piece of data—the exact discount price.

So this morning, when she arrived at work, the special promotion was not yet listed on the home page, and now she has another e-mail from her boss: "Keeping schedules," the boss writes, "is a big part of this job."

Angela feels the rebuke is unfair because she's always reliable—well, almost always.

What's Inside

Using a Personal Planning Calendar

Can you see what Angela was lacking? Although she has a mental list of her commitments and a memo about this particular task, she apparently has no regular calendar or planner where she can write due dates and list her priorities for each day. It's not surprising, then, that she'll sometimes forget.

To make full use of the planning skills you studied in Workshop 8, you need an easy, convenient way to keep track of what is supposed to happen when. There are many such tools available, ranging from pocket calendars to electronic organizers and desktop software. Some people favor a calendar that has specific slots for each half hour of every day; others like a more open format, basically a blank space with the date on it. Some experts argue for "month-at-a-glance" calendars that help you see weeks to come as easily as the current week.

Whatever style of calendar/planner you choose, here are some tips for maximizing your benefits:

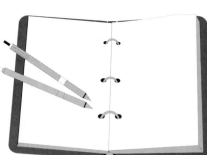

- Use just *one* calendar for all your activities—work, school, home. Multiple calendars invite confusion.
- Keep your calendar with you wherever you go.
- Don't let your days become too crowded. Schedule quiet times, and write them in on the calendar. Also write in your times for recreation, social activities, and so on.
- Highlight the most important entries: for instance, circle them in a bright color or write them in capitals.
- If your calendar or planner has room for notes, use it to record important ideas that occur to you. In this way you'll have all such notes in one place, rather than scribbled on miscellaneous scraps of paper that could easily get lost.
- Likewise, if you choose a calendar with a section for phone numbers, use it to keep important numbers handy.
- Check your calendar at the beginning of each week to see if it needs updating.

Did you know

The ancient Egyptians were the first people to develop a calendar based on the solar year—the time it takes the earth to revolve around the sun.

Analyzing Your Daily Scheduling Problems

Think about some recent times when you had a scheduling problem or conflict: for instance, times when you were late for an appointment; when you forgot to do something; when a deadline sneaked up on you faster than you expected; or when you somehow agreed to be in two places at the same time. List these instances below and decide how the regular use of a planning calendar could help you resolve such problems. If you already have a calendar, how could you improve your use of it?

Scheduling Problems	How I Could Have Avoided Them
1. _____	_____
2. _____	_____
3. _____	_____
4. _____	_____
5. _____	_____

Making a Daily To-Do List

As part of your scheduling system, you should begin each day with a *to-do list*—a list of tasks you intend to tackle that day. On Wednesday, for example, you may have to return four phone calls, finish a report that's due on Thursday, take the first step on a project due next month, consult your supervisor about your vacation plans, and so on. Without making a list, you're likely to forget one of these items.

Each day's to-do list should take into account the needs of your schedule and the amount you've accomplished on preceding days. If your planning calendar has space, you can write your to-do list there. If not, you can use a separate sheet of paper or note card—but stick to one list for each day.

Your to-do list should reflect your deadlines and priorities. Generally you'll want to handle tasks of the highest priority first. When those are done, you can begin on tasks of less priority. If you don't manage to finish all the low-priority items on a particular day, don't worry. If they're important, they'll move up in priority the next day.

> There's a time for some things, and a time for all things; a time for great things, and a time for small things.
>
> —Miguel de Cervantes

If you have a lot of projects, you can use a combination letter-number system for assigning priorities. For instance, use the letter "A" for all tasks that absolutely have to be done today. Use "B" for tasks of lesser importance, "C" for still less crucial tasks, and so on. Then, within each letter category, use the numerals 1, 2, and 3 to rank the items:

Category A	**Tasks I Must Do Today**
A.1	Most important task
A.2	Second-most-important task
A.3	_____
A.4	_____

Category B	**Tasks I Should Start as Soon as Possible**
B.1	_____
B.2	_____
B.3	_____
B.4	_____

Category C	**Tasks I Need to Do Sometime**
C.1	_____
C.2	_____
C.3	_____
C.4	_____

Adapt your to-do list to your own work style. Some people can be comfortable with a to-do list of 25 items! For many of us, though, our eyes tend to glaze when we see more than five or six. Since your to-do list is revised every day, you can make it as short as necessary to keep yourself productive and focused. Just remember what you learned in Workshop 3 about the difference between "urgent" and "important." You have to schedule your work on important long-term tasks so that they aren't constantly shoved aside by short-term urgencies.

THINGS TO DO TODAY

Creating a To-Do List

Create your to-do list for tomorrow. First think about the tasks you must accomplish and how much you can reasonably get done in a single day. List all the tasks that you plan to do tomorrow:

_____   _____

_____   _____

_____   _____

_____   _____

_____   _____

_____   _____

Now consider urgency and importance. Using the combination letter-number system, rank the tasks in the order in which you will handle them.

A.1_____

A.2_____

A.3_____

A.4_____

B.1 _____

B.2 _____

B.3 _____

B.4 _____

C.1 _____

C.2 _____

C.3 _____

C.4 _____

Using Your Peak Productivity Time

Are you a night person who has trouble getting started in the morning? Or are you raring to go at 7:30 A.M. but ready for a snooze by 4:00 in the afternoon?

We all have differences in our peak productivity times. Part of smart scheduling is to recognize your best working times and take advantage of them. If you schedule a hard task for a time when you're sagging, you're likely to struggle with it, wasting your effort and maybe doing a poor job. Likewise, if you spend your most productive time of the day filing papers or buying paper clips, you've lost an opportunity to accomplish something more significant.

Though your work or classes won't always be scheduled to match your highest-energy hours, understanding when you are the most productive will help you get the most out of your time.

When the time is right

Besides using your peak time to best advantage, here are some other tips for scheduling the right time for a task:

✓ Make your telephone calls either early in the day or late in the day, when the people you're calling are least likely to be out of the office or in meetings.

✓ Schedule your lunch for an off-hour, such as 11:00 or 1:00. You'll have a quiet time at work while others are at lunch, and then when you do take lunch, you'll find shorter lines at cafeterias and restaurants.

✓ Schedule appointments for slightly unusual times, such as 2:15 rather than 2:00. You'll find that the people you're meeting are less likely to forget.

✓ For meetings involving several people, begin in late morning. If people are getting hungry for lunch, the meeting won't likely drag on.

Scheduling Productive Times

Identifying Your Productive Times

When are you at your most productive? Is there a single time of day when you are best able to tackle a large or difficult job? Or maybe a couple of times, such as mid-morning and early afternoon? On the lines below, identify your most productive hours:

My Most Productive Times of Day

A.M.   P.M.

_____   _____

_____   _____

_____   _____

Making a Schedule

In the chart below, list ten things you need to do in the next week. Mark with an "X" whether they are easy or hard. Then decide on the appropriate time of day for working on each task. Try to schedule the hard ones for your own peak productivity times.

Things to Do	Easy	Hard	Best Time to Do Task
1.			
2.			
3.			
4.			
5.			
6.			
7.			
8.			
9.			
10.			

Tickler Systems

Often, for long-term projects, you'll manage to remember the big dates, but you'll find small intermediate deadlines easy to forget.

Say you're working with Gene and Marcy on a multipart project. Your work depends on theirs. You begin by completing as much as you can by yourself, but then you have to wait for input from them. They say they'll get back to you, so you set the project aside. As the project deadline approaches, you still haven't heard from them. Frantically you phone them to see what's up. It would have been better, you realize, if you'd called them the week before.

Or imagine that you have an important meeting or interview scheduled for early morning on the 22nd. You have it written on your calendar for that day, but you don't notice it until that very morning, and when you arrive at the meeting you feel unprepared. You wish you'd remembered to take an hour or so the day before to collect your thoughts and review the background information.

For situations like these, you need a systematic method of reminding yourself. Some people create a system by making notes on their planning calendars. If they schedule a meeting with Ms. Ramirez for the 22nd, for example, they also make a calendar note for the 21st: "Prepare for tomorrow's meeting with Ms. Ramirez." Likewise, if they send a memo to Henry and ask for a response within a week, they make an immediate note on next week's calendar: "Call Henry if no response about Project X."

A more elaborate method is to set up a *tickler file*. A typical tickler file is an accordion-like file folder with a separate compartment or folder for each day of the month. The advantage of a tickler file, compared with a regular calendar, is that you can include additional information. For example, to prepare for the meeting with Ms. Ramirez on the 22nd, you'd put a reminder under the 21st and attach the papers you wanted to review.

When you make your to-do list for each day, your tickler file is the first thing to consult. Some people prepare a large, open box with a tickler file for each month of the coming year.

31					
26	27	28		29	30
21	22	23		24	25
16	17	18		19	20
11	12	13		14	15
6	7	8		9	10
1	2	3		4	5
		March			
26	27	28			
21	22	23		24	25
16	17	18		19	20
11	12	13		14	15
6	7	8		9	10
1	2	3		4	5
		February			
31					
26	27	28		29	30
21	22	23		24	25
16	17	18		19	20
11	12	13		14	15
6	7	8		9	10
1	2	3		4	5
		January			

Tickling Yourself

For practice in using a tickler system, think of some events coming up in the next month for which you will need reminders. If you have a report due on the 17th, for instance, you may need to remind yourself to begin your final draft by the 15th. Or if you have a party on the 28th, maybe you could use a reminder to get your hair cut the weekend before.

Use the lines below to identify several such tasks or events. For each one, write in the final date—that is, the date when the event will happen or when the task must be completed. Then indicate what you need to be reminded to do and pick a "tickle" date when you will jog your memory.

Task or Event	Final Date	Reminder Needed	"Tickle" Date
Meeting with Mr. A.	_May 15_	_Review questions to ask_	_May 14_

> **My memory is excellent. I remember everything I need to, exactly one day late.**
>
> —Sam Gridley

GETTING CONNECTED

Many Internet sites now offer free Web-based calendars on which you can record your personal schedule. To keep your information private, you have to sign up with a user name and password, but then you can access your calendar on-line whenever you like. Look at one or two Web calendars and see which features would be most useful for you. Is there an automatic reminder or "tickler" option?

As this book went to press, these were some of the sites offering free calendars:

Calendarz: **http://www.calendarz.com/**
Day-Timer Digital: **http://digital.daytimer.com/**
MyTime: **http://mytime.lycos.com/mytime**
Netscape Netcenter: **http://www.netscape.com/**
OpenCal: **http://www.opencal.com/**
When.com: **http://www.when.com/**
Yahoo!: **http://www.yahoo.com/**

You can also do a Web search with a phrase like *free web calendar*.

WORKSHOP WRAP-UP

- For effective planning and scheduling, you should use a convenient calendar that you can keep with you wherever you go.
- A daily to-do list, clearly organized by priority, keeps you on track each day.
- Different people have different peak productivity times. You can schedule your hardest tasks for the times when you're best able to cope with them.
- Finally, good scheduling requires a "tickler" system to give you reminders at appropriate times.

Checklist for Self–Management and Goal Setting

✓ Identify your long-term goals and define them in clear terms.

✓ Write a personal mission statement.

✓ Rank your long-term goals in order of importance and decide when you hope to achieve each one.

✓ Take full advantage of your daily experiences to make progress toward your goals.

✓ Divide your long-term goals into specific, shorter-term goals.

✓ Set a timetable for each short-term goal.

✓ Do something every day toward achieving your goals.

✓ Prioritize your tasks on the basis of importance and urgency.

✓ Reduce time spent on urgent but unimportant tasks.

✓ Resist the "rush" of crisis mode; make time for more important goals.

✓ Take time to get organized, beginning with your desk or workspace.

✓ Learn to screen documents quickly and file them efficiently.

✓ Control interruptions, such as telephone calls and unwanted visitors.

✓ When appropriate, say "no," politely but firmly.

✓ When possible, delegate tasks and responsibilities to others.

✓ Use "scraps" of time wisely.

✓ Aim for high quality in your work, not for an unnecessary degree of perfection.

✓ Be decisive.

✓ Confront problems head-on rather than losing time by worrying.

✓ Recognize and understand your procrastination tendencies.

✓ Break the procrastination habit by striving to modify both your behavior and your negative thoughts.

✓ Make time for planning. Divide each big task into small steps, put the steps in the right order, and set a deadline for each.

✓ Put your plans in writing and make revisions as needed.

✓ To improve your planning effectiveness, work to develop your skill in estimating the time that tasks will require.

✓ Use a personal calendar for planning and scheduling.

✓ Make a daily to-do list, organized by priority.

✓ Schedule difficult tasks during your most productive times.

✓ Use a "tickler" system for schedule and deadline reminders.

Time-Management Tools

For your convenience, the following pages offer blank forms that you can use to work on your time-management skills.

My Time Log

List how you spend your time for an entire day. Then go back and rate the activities by priority (with 1 as the highest priority and 5 as the lowest). Add comments about how you could manage your time better.

Time (start/finish)	Activity	Priority	Comments

My Time Conflicts

Week of _____

During one week, list in the "Conflict" column the times when two or more demanding tasks conflict with each other. At the end of the week, look back and analyze how you handled the conflicts and write a summary in the "How I Handled It" column. Then use the far-right column for reflections on improvements you can make. Can you rethink your priorities, for instance? Delegate more tasks? Control interruptions better?

	Conflict	How I Handled It	Ways to Improve My Time Management
Monday			
Tuesday			
Wednesday			
Thursday			
Friday			

Time-Management Tools

Monday

8:00 _____

_____

9:00 _____

_____

10:00 _____

_____

11:00 _____

_____

12:00 _____

_____

1:00 _____

_____

2:00 _____

_____

3:00 _____

_____

4:00 _____

_____

5:00 _____

_____

6:00 _____

_____

7:00 _____

_____

Tuesday

8:00 _____

_____

9:00 _____

_____

10:00 _____

_____

11:00 _____

_____

12:00 _____

_____

1:00 _____

_____

2:00 _____

_____

3:00 _____

_____

4:00 _____

_____

5:00 _____

_____

6:00 _____

_____

7:00 _____

_____

Wednesday

8:00 _____

_____

9:00 _____

_____

10:00 _____

_____

11:00 _____

_____

12:00 _____

_____

1:00 _____

_____

2:00 _____

_____

3:00 _____

_____

4:00 _____

_____

5:00 _____

_____

6:00 _____

_____

7:00 _____

_____

Thursday

8:00 _____

_____

9:00 _____

_____

10:00 _____

_____

11:00 _____

_____

12:00 _____

_____

1:00 _____

_____

2:00 _____

_____

3:00 _____

_____

4:00 _____

_____

5:00 _____

_____

6:00 _____

_____

7:00 _____

_____

Time-Management Tools

Friday

8:00 _____

_____

9:00 _____

_____

10:00 _____

_____

11:00 _____

_____

12:00 _____

_____

1:00 _____

_____

2:00 _____

_____

3:00 _____

_____

4:00 _____

_____

5:00 _____

_____

6:00 _____

_____

7:00 _____

_____

To Do

Date		
Priority	Activity	Complete

To Do

Date		
Priority	Activity	Complete

To Do

Date		
Priority	**Activity**	**Complete**

To Do

Date		
Priority	Activity	Complete

Time-Management Tools

To Do

Date		
Priority	Activity	Complete

Also in the
QUICK SKILLS SERIES

Attitude and Self-Esteem

Decision Making and Problem Solving

Listening

Speaking and Presenting

Reading in the Workplace

Writing in the Workplace

For information on new titles:
call 1-800-354-9706
or visit us on-line at
www.swep.com

5886